CRICKET TEAS

Phil McCann

AMBERLEY

About the Author

Phil McCann is an author and cricket enthusiast. Happiest when sampling cakes before a cricket tea, he is an expert in washing-up and commenting on the moisture content of Victoria sponges. He has weaknesses for well-executed cut shots and traditional oat flapjacks. Phil also grows award-winning vegetables.

Dedicated to Catherine,
Jack and Freddie.

Cover image courtesy of Ian R. Ward Illustration.

First published 2019

Amberley Publishing
The Hill, Stroud
Gloucestershire, GL5 4EP

www.amberley-books.com

British Library Cataloguing in Publication Data.
A catalogue record for this book is available from the British Library.

ISBN 978 1 4456 9322 4 (paperback)
ISBN 978 1 4456 9323 1 (ebook)

Typeset in 10pt on 13pt Sabon.
Typesetting and Origination by Amberley Publishing.
Printed in the UK.

Contents

Foreword 4

Putting the Ts in Introduction 5

1 Putting the T in History 10

2 Putting the T in Tea-Makers 28

3 Putting the Ts in Tea-Takers 49

4 Putting the T in Favourites 67

5 Putting the Ts in Etiquette 74

6 Putting the T in Victory 85

Acknowledgements 95

With Thanks 96

Foreword

If there's one thing that everyone knows about *Test Match Special*, it is that we do know about teas. In particular, we know about cakes.

This expertise came to the attention of nPower, during the time they were sponsors of Test cricket in England. It seemed to them the perfect blend. After all, what good is all that electricity except to put the kettle on? So they married up *TMS* and the tea interval for a 'Tea Lady of the Year' competition. (That would be frowned upon in these egalitarian times, I know. We did have one gentleman competitor, as I remember.)

And who better to be our adjudicator than the former England captain and legend in his own tea interval – Mike Gatting. I am not sure that sampling the entries did anything to lessen Gatt's increasing similarity to Henry VIII, but it was a jolly feature – if a nightmare for a producer to organise live on the air. It was not helped, either, when our presenter, Johnny Saunders, invited Mike to comment on Mrs Smith's baps. The hysteria that followed may have helped to end this programme idea.

The introduction of cake into the commentary box can really be attributed to the late Brian Johnston. One day, back in the 1970s, a lady sent him a chocolate cake. Being well brought up, naturally he thanked her. Encouraged by this, that night, in kitchens across the land, sleeves were rolled up and cake production started on a scale to put *The Great British Bake Off* to shame. Thereafter, the more he thanked our baking listeners, the greater the output became. In the interests of our waistlines, I discovered the whereabouts of all children's hospitals in the vicinity of each Test ground and made regular deliveries.

In Colombo in 1993, the Military Attaché at the British High Commission kindly brought a chocolate cake to the *TMS* box. I think he must have imagined we were in air-conditioned luxury in temperatures approaching 40 degrees. We were not and his generosity left us scooping up a chocolate puddle with teaspoons.

Our best cake delivery, though, came in 2001, when Her Majesty the Queen delivered a magnificent Dundee cake to us at Lord's. She seemed slightly incredulous as she handed it to me, saying, 'They tell me people give you cakes.'

It is a far cry to that from the lavish teas produced every summer weekend in village cricket pavilions all over the land. In each league everyone knows which clubs produce the best teas and I know of village teams who have employed local farmers' wives to cater for them and boost their reputations. There is nothing new about this. More than a hundred years ago, W. G. Grace declared that Moreton-in-Marsh had the best teas in Gloucestershire, if not in all of England.

Whether savoury or sweet is better, or one followed by the other, I will leave to the discerning cricketer. This book may well help his or her decision.

Peter Baxter, producer of *Test Match Special* (1973–2007)

Putting the Ts in Introduction

A cricket tea is an integral part of any cricket match. It's a well-known fact that some players only turn out at windswept grounds on the promise of a solid brew, chewy wedge of cake and a sticky handful of noxious egg sandwiches. Captains of village cricket teams know full well that when the fixture list is posted to the noticeboard at the start of the season, some matches will be oversubscribed with players. The promise of a sumptuous, pillowy bap filled with rough-grated, tangy, mature Cheddar cheese and crunchy coleslaw is simply too tempting for many an aspiring middle order all-rounder. Dates for family holidays have been known to change once team selection has been finalised.

Likewise, there is always an occasional away fixture where the teas are traditionally so dire that soft tissue injury-inspired limps suspiciously appear so that players, usually fast bowlers, can avoid selection and steer well clear of a highly refined yet undefined meat paste cob.

The simple appearance of cricket teas on trestle tables at thousands of grounds around the world hardly pays testament to the many dedicated stalwarts of cricket cuisine. Scribbled on the back of a grubby used envelope, the cricket teas rota is the last match day chore to be completed. Staffing the bar, putting out boundary markers and clearing the outfield of offensive detritus usually beats doing the teas by a country mile. Yet, teas get done. Names are unceremoniously jotted against vacant fixtures, causing captains to sigh with relief in the comforting knowledge that all is well in the world. These are the unsung heroes of the club, for without these cricket tea makers you, your club, the county players benefitting from your support and all of our international heroes would flag in the fortieth over or feel faint charging in during the fiftieth.

Nutrition, however, does change markedly from most village cricket clubs to the more elite international venues across the world. Village cricketers traditionally assess their teas on sugar content and sheer density of the offering. 'If it's heavy it'll be good' is a good yardstick to club teas. And, of course, it must all be piled onto one plate as no one wants to be caught in that nightmare scenario of re-approaching the tea table for sweet treats to find them snaffled by the opposition wicketkeeper, a rotund fellow at the best of times.

International players are measured not necessarily in their enthusiasm for the tea table but rather for what they take on board. Carbohydrates, proteins and fats are all forensically calculated. Fruit, a scarcity at village grounds, is often involved. Calories constitute the key figures alongside run and strike rates, bowling stats and on rainy days, D, L and their new friend S. Cricket is both a numbers and letters game.

At the end of a satisfying day's play, still buzzing with excitement on the drive home, the talk between teammates will always turn to the cricket tea. Years down the track, few can remember an expansive slog sweep for six, but most can reminisce about the moisture content of a specific Victoria sponge at a particular ground on a definite date.

Or, perish the thought, shuddering flashbacks to a cricket tea where the sandwiches weren't cut into triangles.

Each and every cricketer, from village occasional to adored international, can recall the ground where they've experienced a superb tea or where disappointment in a spread tarnished a maiden century, tainted a diving slip catch or even marred a fifer. Cricket teas are important; much more important than many people realise.

Just ask any cricketer.

Always bowl first then sit back and enjoy the tea.
'Don't mind if I do.'

My Favourite Cricket Tea

Sir Michael Parkinson is best known as a broadcaster, author and journalist. He also loves cricket. He needs no other introduction.

The beauty of cricket teas when I was a kid was that they were in a time before we were obsessed with diet, body fat, calorie excess or demands created by a vegan diet. What you got was a big slice of white bread, a lot of butter – margarine had been invented but we couldn't afford it – and a slice of ham which could have been used as a shin pad in soccer season. All you wanted to do after that was to lie down in the outfield and fall asleep.

But the most memorable part of our tea in those distant days – I am talking late 1940s, early 1950s – was the tea, not so much the black liquid in pint pots but the big brown metal teapot itself. This was provided by a large, jolly woman who lived in the next street to us who was much in demand throughout the year at funerals when the biggest teapot in the village was required. Her advertising stated – 'cricket teas and funerals a speciality.'

Otherwise the only real memory I have of cricket teas is much later after I had moved down south where things were a bit more refined – salmon paste sandwiches and plump fruit cake – because it wasn't so much the food that drew my attention as the appetite of our scorer – a small but stout woman with a voracious appetite.

As soon as the tea interval approached, she was on her mark in the scoring box and when she saw the umpire removing the bails she burst out of her shed and ran across the field as if this was to be the last meal of her life. There was nothing beautiful about her stride, being functional rather than graceful and designed to get her into the pavilion before the players arrived. She had a formidable appetite and the cricketers had to be sharp and decisive to get their share.

Sir Michael Parkinson CBE, broadcaster; journalist; author and cricket fanatic.

Left: Michael, left-handed bat, kitted out in his dad's flannels and a jumper knitted by his mum.

Below: Michael with Elton John, Peter Cook, Nicholas Parsons and many other celebrity cricketers in the 1970s. Wes Hall, West Indies international, was perhaps the best bowler in the team.

Time for the new cherry.

I

Putting the T in History

It's a fact that, if performed in a manner of professionalism and with 100 per cent effort, most sports make you hungry and thirsty. That's why refreshing and refuelling during the game is vital. Tennis players are forever chomping on over-ripe bananas and guzzling down lukewarm lemon barley water between sets. Footballers all pile into the dressing room for a suck on a quarter of an orange while rugby players don't always make it off the pitch for their glug of water and a slurp at a sachet of energy gel. Cricket – thank goodness – is different.

Victorian tea was the forerunner to the classic cricket tea in England. Australia did it their own way.

Cricket is the only sport where, at around 4 p.m., its participants down tools and walk off the playing arena for a twenty-minute break for tea and sandwiches. And that, remember, is only a few hours after a full lunch has been taken, and that in turn is only around three hours after the start. What a truly beautiful game.

Cricket tea, traditionally taken between 4 p.m. and 4.20 p.m. in first class matches, or at the end of one innings at village club level, undoubtedly has its roots in the Victorian age. As Queen Victoria was putting her name to a rather wonderful cake, the whole idea of afternoon tea was created by Anna, 7th Duchess of Bedford. Its main purpose was to stave off the hunger pangs between lunch and what was fast becoming the fashion for taking a late evening meal. She felt that a light tea of cakes, sandwiches and a drink of tea in the afternoon was the perfect balance. She enjoyed it so much that she simply had to include her friends, and the tradition of afternoon tea soon developed.

This afternoon tea was served on a low table in a lounge where guests could choose their food and place it on their own plate. As this rather gentile performance was playing out before both the hoi polloi and high society, cricket was being played in the searing, singeing wind of Perth's Freemantle Doctor (that's Perth in Australia and not Scotland), under Sydney's blue sky blazing with scorching summer sun and in the melting atmosphere of the MCG. A tea interval was not simply fashionable in such far-flung and exotic places: it was a necessity.

As the Australians were stopping for a tea interval, Victorian high society sipped their tepid tinctures and daintily determined which particular cucumber sandwich was the chosen one. It was a marriage made in cake heaven.

Tea intervals developed and started to infiltrate into English cricket. But not everyone liked the thought of them. In response to a letter he had received decrying tea intervals, former England international Elias Henry 'Patsy' Hendren clearly pointed out in 1924 that, 'When one has been running about the long field all afternoon, a cup of tea is a wonderful 'pick-me-up' as regards myself.' The players liked them, but the controversy raged on.

In 1928, *The Cricketer* magazine reported that 'the tea interval is an unnecessary evil' and that surely 'it is not necessary that a team must all sit down to tea together like a school treat. Could the batting side have tea individually while waiting to go in or after they have got out?' The problem was that the paying public were seeing too many drawn matches due to delays in play. *The Cricketer* goes on to summarise: 'I certainly think that by eliminating this ancient custom of the tea interval, there would be more definite results, and it would give greater satisfaction to those young cricketers who sometimes have to wait weeks before they have an opportunity to bat for their club.'

Sir Home Gordon, a renowned cricket writer, publisher and old Etonian, went even further when writing in the same publication in 1940 by stating that the tea interval was brought over here 'for the special purpose of spinning out the match'.

Sir Home Gordon then detailed his annoyance at a particular game he'd witnessed but also his joy at the splendid tea he had experienced: 'In a country town last Sunday I saw an afternoon match, in which each side batted for an hour and a half with a

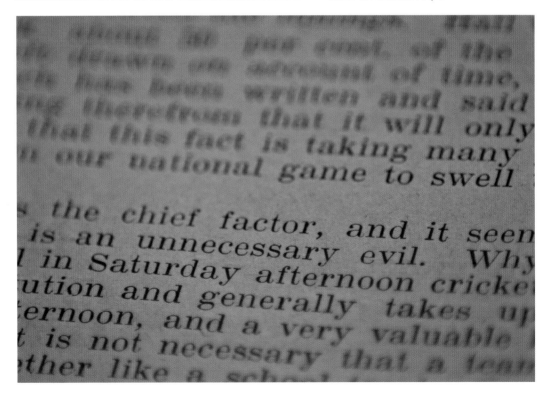

Left: Elias Henry 'Patsy' Hendren of Middlesex and England defended the cricket tea in his response to a spectator's complaint. (Credit: The Roger Mann Picture Library)

Below: *The Cricketer* vehemently opposed cricket teas, branding them 'an unnecessary evil' in 1928.

Right: Food for thought in *The Cricketer*, 1928.

Below: The 'good' old days where players were served their tea, and cigarettes, on the field of play by waiting staff in 1931. The match itself is Gentlemen *v.* Players at the Scarborough Festival.

very elastic half-hour for migration to a neighbouring inn. There a first rate meal, consisting of well-brewed tea, cress sandwiches composed of home-made bread, and slices of plum cake, was obtained for the inclusive and moderate capitation price of eightpence.' That's a decent sounding cricket tea for the equivalent of what would now be around £1.40.

Cricket tea intervals continued with refreshments often being brought out onto the field of play, but soon cricketers were ambling off to the pavilion to enjoy their tasty teatime titbits and, of course, spectators adapted, enjoying their own sandwiches and hot drinks from the ubiquitous tartan flask.

The cricket tea interval will now take some moving. It's as firmly entrenched in the game as sponsorship, floodlights and coloured clothing. All are, of course, superb commercial opportunities for teams.

But there's so much more to a tea interval than twenty minutes of lascivious locustry. For, when faced with extravagant spreads of niblets of desire, cricketers are in fact looking at and tasting a fascinating history of food inexorably entwined with cricket. Twenty minutes is barely enough time to take it all in.

Brewing Up

The drink of tea itself predates cricket by a couple of thousand years. Legend tells of Emperor Shen Nung in China sitting beneath a tree watching his servant boil some water. Remember that this legend is PC (pre-cricket) so there weren't any live games or even highlights of the afternoon session to enjoy at the time.

As this exciting exercise was unfolding, a few leaves of a tree, *Camellia sinensis*, blew into the brew. Obviously the Emperor wanted to know what this accidental broth tasted like and, after a few sips, the drink of tea was born.

Rather than relying on an errant leaf to float down and flutter into the clubhouse kitchen to deposit itself into the warship of a teapot, most clubs now use tea bags to produce the magical mix of theobromine, polyphenols and caffeine.

Teabags are not steeped in too much legend as their arrival is a little bit more recent. In 1908, an American tea merchant called Thomas Sullivan sent out his tea in small packets. The parcels were expertly designed to be opened before brewing. But, in time-honoured fashion, customers ignored any instruction leaflet and instead plunged the whole lot into hot water. From then on, tea bags were created, further developed and eventually reached the UK in the 1950s, around the time that Jim Laker took his legendary nineteen-wicket haul against Australia at Old Trafford.

UK cricket tea makers embraced the little sachets and, by the turn of the millennium, the majority of club brewers were guessing at how many really constituted the correct amount for the industrial-sized tea silo skulking in the corner of the pavilion. The rule of 'one bag per player and one for the pot' does sometimes seem to have gone awry when navigating a mug of tea with a knife and fork.

Conversely, the new brew student may go light on the tea bags and produce a pot of 'fortnight' tea: i.e. it's too weak.

Young shoots of *Camellia sinensis* provide the raw material for every cricketer's favourite brew. It's easy to grow and brew your own.

Every club has its own mystery teabag equation.

Keep it Hot

Spectators at a cricket match often have their tea in a flask. A thermos flask. A thermos flask invented by James Dewar, a Scottish physicist in 1872. His first flask wasn't devised for commercial use at cricket grounds at Alloa, Kelso or Inchture. It was used solely in his own work for keeping gasses cold. Dewar was the first person to make liquid hydrogen.

His double-walled glass vessel had exciting commercial potential and a company called Thermos quickly waded in and brought the invention to the people in 1904.

A stainless steel version was introduced in 1978, preventing breakages at cricket grounds around the world. This was especially useful in the same year at Canterbury as spectators celebrated Kent winning the county championship.

A metal flask of tea is a vital component in a spectator's cricket survival kit.

Sarnie Time

John Monatgu, the 4th Earl of Sandwich, was a keen gambling man and, rather than leaving the card table to dine, he insisted on being fed while dealing out the pack.

He called for slices of meat between two slices of bread to be brought to him so that he could continue his habit of losing money uninterrupted. Fellow gamblers and then friends, acquaintances and the general populace all cottoned on to the barked order of 'bring me what Sandwich wanted'.

This was in around 1762, just as the world-famous cradle of cricket, Hambledon Cricket Club in Hampshire, was becoming established. It only feels right that cricket and its main refreshment were developing hand in glove.

But a sandwich is only called a sandwich because John Montagu was Earl of Sandwich. He could have been an earl of many other places. The cricketer's sandwich could easily have been a corned beef Ramsbottom or a baloney Ballownie. Craving a Craven sir?

It's only a sandwich because he was the Earl of Sandwich. It could easily have been any other place name.

Creamed It

The absolute must-have cake on a cricket tea table is a Victoria sponge. Nothing ignites discussion more than a Victoria sponge. Or is it Victoria sandwich? The filling (raspberry or strawberry?), the additional layer of cream (whipped or none at all?) and even the dusting on top (caster or icing?) all court controversy in cake circles.

Even the history of the cake inflames passionate argument. The easily digestible storyline is that when Queen Victoria tasted the cake she liked it so much that she put her name on it. It's a well-touted and painless explanation.

But plunge the cake fork a little deeper and it's soon discovered that due to the chance of choking, the children in the royal household at the time were banned from eating nuts and seeds. They needed a simple, tasty cake and one that could be cut into small finger-sized portions for eager digits. And it needed to be served around 4 p.m.

It was then that Queen Victoria saw how useful the cake was and nailed her colours to the mast and her name to the cake. All this was happening around the time that Canada was playing the United States in the first official international cricket match.

A case of the Victoria sponge/sandwich and international cricket making their tottering first steps to the cricket tea table in tandem.

Victoria sponge or sandwich? Jam and cream? A dusting of icing sugar or not? When will the arguing stop?

Ketch It

If you proffer hotdogs to your cricketers at teatime then you have to provide ketchup. It's cricket law. Actually, whatever you dish up at the tea interval, there will be one or two players who want to slather 'Tommy K' all over it.

Ketchup has a history shrouded in mystery but most food historians agree that the present-day offering is based on a pickled fish sauce originating in China in the seventeenth century. It doesn't sound too appetising.

Ketchup underwent various recipe changes until, in 1837, a chap called Jonas Yerkes started selling bottles of his own mashup in the USA. In 1876, Heinz developed their tomato-based ketchup. People quite liked it. All this was happening as Americans had one eye on the fiftieth birthday of baseball and another on the fast developing game of cricket and the proposal by its governing body to introduce a declaration rule where one side could decide that they had enough runs to win.

Nowadays, more than 650 million bottles of Heinz tomato ketchup are sold worldwide each year (not just to village cricket clubs) and that declaration rule is used to great effect in many county and international games. Not so much in limited over matches on a wet May bank holiday in Grimsby though.

The only danger of tomato ketchup at a cricket tea is the unfortunate violent expulsion of the Master of Stain from the bottle onto white cricket kit. The ketchup kings at Heinz insist that ketchup should naturally – using gravity and gravity

Tommy K is a vital ingredient to a successful cricket tea, no matter what's on the plate.

alone – exit the iconic glass bottle at 0.028 mph. Anything faster and it's rejected. This is fine under normal circumstances.

However, this is way too slow for a number two batsman gearing up for an innings of a lifetime by shovelling high-density foodstuffs into his face before facing a couple of throwdowns from the number eleven batter armed with half a kilo of quiche.

A firm smack on the base of a glass ketchup bottle is always the tried and trusted method of hurrying the tea queue up. Cricketers should always hold a finger over the top or cap of any container of ketchup before enthusiastically shaking to mix the contents. Plastic squeezy containers are the most dangerous.

And is it too much to ask that all players wipe clean the top before clipping or screwing the lid back on? Yes, it is. Another law of cricket to adhere to.

Keep off the Square

What a cake! Every cricket tea table needs a slab of the iconic square sweet stuff. The addictive mix of light sponge, in two colours, apricot jam glue and a marzipan duvet makes Battenberg the go-to cake for cricketers.

Its history is as chequered as the cake itself. Several stories and legends are trotted out when discussing this cake at the tea interval. The first and most popular is that it was named in honour of the marriage between Princess Victoria and Prince Louis of Battenberg in 1884. The tale goes on to say that the quarters seen in the cake refer to the four Battenberg princes.

A firm favourite with cricketers around the country. 'Quarters' is favourite, but a nine-square version is possible.

However, recipes abound both before and after that date for a nine-squared chequered cake along with versions of the quartered look. Some also include a generous coating of desiccated coconut.

This whole grey area of cake history is totally understandable as attention in 1884 was somewhat distracted from the refreshments, flowers and dress of that particular royal wedding. A three-match series was being played between England against Australia with matches at Lords, the Oval and Old Trafford, and possibly bricks of that new-fangled cake, Battenberg, were being noshed in the stands. It must have been an exciting time as England won the series 1-0.

For modern-day cricketers, Battenberg is usually four-square unless an ambitious have-a-go hero home baker has attempted the nine-square version. It's a difficult cake to bake so chances are it's the mass-produced version, first churned out by bakeries from around the Second World War and now gracing cricket tea tables up and down the UK and beyond.

Hard Luck

Two notable dates stand out when it comes to that doyenne of a cricket tea table, Jaffa Cakes. First up is 1927. Lancashire won the championship title; New Zealand toured England; Douglas Jardine and Harold Larwood were limbering up by topping the batting and bowling averages respectively; and Jaffa Cakes were

Wear the badge with pride. Jaffa Cakes are essential in a cricket tea.

introduced to the UK. It would be difficult to choose the BBC Sports Personality of the Year if it was in existence back then. A light, cakey base, thin layer of tangerine jam and a topping of chocolate all combine to produce the perfect shop-bought accompaniment to a cricket tea.

However, in 1991, Jaffa Cakes had the indignity of being dragged through the courts. As Essex were winning the championship, Sri Lanka were touring England and Carl Hooper and Waqar Younis were topping the batting and bowling averages respectively, Jaffa Cakes were in the witness box, having to prove whether they were cakes or biscuits. The case revolved around tax.

The significance of the borderline between cakes and biscuits is that a cake is zero-rated even if it is covered in chocolate, whereas a biscuit is standard-rated if wholly or partly covered in chocolate or some product similar in taste and appearance. Customs and Excise decided to review the case of Jaffa Cakes. Jaffa Cakes had always been classified as non-VATable items but, following a review, the department reversed its view of the liability. Jaffa Cakes were then ruled to be biscuits partly covered in chocolate and standard-rated.

Panic in pavilions around the world ensued. United Biscuits (as McVities, one of the largest manufacturers of Jaffa Cakes) appealed against this decision. Big money was at stake. Hours of 'm'luds', 'call the next witness' and 'silence in the courts' could have been avoided by asking any passing cricketer or cricket tea maker. It transpired that the answer was simple. When left in the open air, cakes turn hard whereas biscuits go soft. And surely the clue is in the name. Jaffa Cakes are classed as cake, are rightfully designated a staple foodstuff and are thankfully still within the budget of tea makers in village cricket clubs.

Crumbs of Comfort

1985 was a great year for cricket. The Ashes were regained by England; Leicestershire won the Benson & Hedges Cup; India won the World Championship in Australia; and one particular item on the cricket tea table was introduced to the public. Hobnobs were a hit the moment they were placed on the cricket tea table.

'One nibble and you're nobbled' was on the lips of many cricketers around the tea table. As were the crumbs. Based on oats, and therefore deemed by many cricketers to be healthy, they were devoured by the packet. It was quickly discovered, mostly by umpires, that although Hobnobs were perfect for eating dry, they were even more delicious when slightly moistened after a good old dunk in a mug of top quality, strongly stewed tea. A platefull at the tea interval made all the torrid appeals and scowls from the bowlers so much easier to stomach.

Two years later, as Australia were beating England in the Cricket World Cup and Nottinghamshire were winning the county championship, a chocolate-covered version of the Hobnob was unleashed upon the unsuspecting cricket-loving and wider public. This younger stripling of the original favourite is also perfect for eating dry but requires a slightly more skilled dunker to get the full benefit of this

'Just the one. Oh, go on then, I'll have another.' An umpire's favourite when dunked with care.

marvellous creation. It's only a manoeuvre that fully accredited ECB ACO umpires should ever attempt.

Chocolate Hobnobs definitely require a highly educated expert in health to ease them through the nutrition police. Thankfully such custodians of justice are already dunking and dipping to their hearts' content. They are usually the people in white coats, straining black trousers and sporting a wide-brimmed hat.

Clinging on for the Draw

Clingfilm is an essential tool in the cricket tea maker's kitchen. Plates of sandwiches, biscuits, cakes and quiches all need covering from inquisitive flies, wasps and other summer irritants such as rapacious groundstaff. Cricket tea makers first got their hands on the stuff in 1953 as England were regaining The Ashes, Surrey were being crowned county championship winners and Berkshire topped the Minor Counties League. And many of those tea makers have still got that very first square of clingfilm on their hands to this day. Curse that static.

It was an accidental find in the laboratories at Dow Chemicals in the USA that started the clingfilm revolution. At first, it was used as a protective covering and was often sprayed onto aircraft and car upholstery. A few changes in its chemical makeup allowed clingfilm to be introduced into the food industry and now rolls of it tangle and frustrate cricket tea makers every season.

Extreme ball tampering or clingfilm just doing what it does best – clinging to everything except plates of cricket tea food?

However, there are two ways to reduce your stress levels when attempting to use it. Firstly, keep your clingfilm in the fridge. Secondly, wet your fingers before using clingfilm. Both tricks will make protecting your bloomers and oven-bottoms from spidery fingers so much easier and may even buy you some extra time and allow you to see an over or two of play.

Easy Pickings

Every cricketer loves a homemade cake, but unfortunately not every cricket club has a baker on its books. And sometimes a little factory-made, prepacked amuse-bouche is just the ticket to tickle your fancy. A French one perhaps?

Mr Kipling claims he makes exceedingly good cakes and thousands of cricketers agree. Perhaps it is because they fit into most mouths in one go. Or maybe it's due to the fact they look great on a three-tiered cake stand. It was back in 1967 that a range of mass-produced, bakery quality cakes arrived in brightly coloured boxes in corner shops and supermarkets around the UK. It didn't take long before they were being offered up to cricketers at village clubs.

French Fancies were the stoic opener in a tenacious cake line-up, with thousands of cricketers gorging themselves on the new sweet treat. The soft sponge, teasing blob of buttercream, overcoat of icing and the ornamental drizzle were too much for many an ordinarily conservative point fielder. They became silly on the effects.

Slight finger pressure on the cake enables easier access through the grill with minimum wastage.

But while paper doilies were being rinsed, dried and stored for use on another match day, debate raged over the flavour of the various colours of French Fancy in the box: yellow = lemon-flavoured; brown = chocolate-flavoured; and pink = strangely plain?

As all this was happening in village club pavilions around the country, Yorkshire were busy winning the county championship (again) and Ken Barrington and Derek Underwood were topping the batting and bowling league tables. What a year to be part of cricket.

My Favourite Cricket Tea

Aberdeen-born Kyle Coetzer is the captain of the men's Scotland cricket team and is widely regarded as the best batsman ever produced by the country. Averaging forty runs in One Day Internationals, it came as no surprise to many when, in June 2018, he helped mastermind the defeat of England in a thrilling fifty-over match at The Grange in Edinburgh.

Cricket Scotland's thistle is worn with pride and invokes passion within the Scottish team.

Kyle Coetzer masterminded Scotland's sensational victory over England in 2018. Some say it was the greatest One Day International of that year.

He's also played for Durham CCC, Northamptonshire CCC and Chittagong Kings in Bangladesh, but it's back at his village club where he fondly remembers the cricket teas.

I played with my dad and brothers at Stoneywood Dyce Cricket Club in Aberdeen so the only way my mum would see us at the weekend was by being at the ground making the teas. The great thing with that was she knew exactly what we liked, so that's what we got.

I think there has to be a simplicity to a tea break and you really have to like what is presented. Good solid sandwiches never fail. Quiches are great because you don't have to wait and now pizzas and hotdogs are often on the table at village grounds. No one wants to be hanging around in a queue waiting for tea, especially if you have to get out and warm up to bowl the first over, and that's why scones, and I love them, should already have the jam on them. It saves vital seconds.

What about cakes? Everyone loves a cake at a cricket tea.

Apple pies and jam doughnuts are my favourite. But saying that, whenever I played at Forfarshire Cricket Club in Broughty Ferry the teas were magnificent. Absolutely superb. They had everything – sandwiches, salads, quiches, pasta, Eton mess, cakes, the works. Nothing could compare to that spread. Not even my mum's.

A tough choice but two down, three across has to be a winner.

2

Putting the T in Tea-Makers

There is no doubt that a cricket tea maker is the cornerstone of a successful cricket club. Without one, two or even a throbbing committee of tea makers, a club quickly slides into a sordid afternoon of prepacked meal deals and plastic-shrouded, saccharin-saturated cake-like guff. Or even worse – players having to provide their own teas.

That's plum.

Cricket tea makers have plenty to think about when planning and preparing a cricket tea. A few pointers to becoming a true Trojan of the cricket tea world include:

Quantity

Quantity is vital as an empty tea table encircled by snarling, salivating cricketers is the seed of nightmares to tea makers. Tea makers usually need to cater for twenty-two players, two umpires and two scorers. Then, depending on the fixture, any amount of casual onlookers may join in along with passers-by and local itinerants in search of a sustaining sarnie. If any of the above are disappointed it will lead to the matter being brought up at the next committee meeting as a named and numbered item and not languishing in AOB. This is usually highlighted by the committee member who missed out on a glob of Eton mess.

Go large, overdo quantities and, once the players and officials have trundled back to the pitch, charge everyone else approaching the remains of the spread. This will raise vital coffers for the following week's tea.

Quality

Quality is paramount. Anyone can buy a cheap loaf of plasticised white bread, smear chemical goo on the slices and drop on shavings of mechanically retrieved meat of unknown origin. But not a cricket tea stalwart. Redoubtable cricket tea makers do things better.

Quality doesn't have to cost the earth. Don't be afraid to ask local businesses for free produce to use in your cricket tea. In return for a small card saying 'With thanks to' on the tea table, many butchers, bakers and – if you are really pushing the boat out and trying to impress – the local candlestick makers are only too happy to slip a gratis sausage, buckshee baguette or a complimentary pricket into your bag.

Don't be Late

Tea makers need to be on time with the spread. There is nothing more irritating to players than a tea in a premature state of completion. Now, this takes a mixing bowl of skill as a flurry of wickets late on in an innings will bring a tea forward from any pre-planned time. Likewise, a sharp shower of rain can curtail an innings, bring about those dreaded words from an umpire, 'let's take tea early', and throw your curly fries into a proper spin. You can of course negate all of these scenarios by being prepared.

Preparation

Benjamin Franklin may never have actually whipped up a strawberry meringue with fresh cream, but he was spot on when he said, 'By failing to prepare, you are preparing to fail.' There are three phases of cricket tea preparation:

Pretty sure that tea will be called early. Cricket tea makers need to watch the weather.

Extreme Preparation

This can mean putting the whole of the cricket tea in the pavilion the evening before the match. However, preparing the tea so early only results in the challenge of guarding the tea from nocturnal animals such as owls, mice and groundstaff. Owls shouldn't be a problem if whoever was last in the clubhouse actually shut all of the windows, and mice can be deterred by persuading the club cat to actually do its job, but no tea maker can 100 per cent guard against the shenanigans of a prowling Green Man.

Reasonable Preparation

This involves making most of the sandwiches and quiches the night before, storing them at home and delivering to the pavilion on the morning of the match. However, this presents the worry of guarding against home-grown nocturnal animals such as pets, children and partners. Pets can be trained to stay away and children can be put to bed early with a copy of the *Wisden Almanac* of their birth year. Partners are more difficult to control.

Just in Time

This often involves making items on the morning of the match and delivering an hour or so before the tea is due. This is the most popular of preparation tactics and there is always the guarantee that players will help you unload the individual plates, platters and bowls from the car. Be mindful that this is not because they are being polite and helpful. They are not 'nice young chaps' nor are they a credit to their parents. Far

Right: Danger lurks when preparing a cricket tea at home.

Below: Macaroons are a top target when moving a cricket tea from the boot of a car to the pavilion.

from it. Be in no doubt that all the players are doing is having a sneaky look at the tea before it hits the table. This may initiate thoughts of some pre-match pilfering.

Remember that a *Wisden Almanac* will not only send young children to sleep, but will also cause damage when slammed onto fingers that are straying furtively around your macaroons. Use this weapon wisely, especially if the potential pre-match pilferer is your own wicketkeeper. Or spin bowler. Or opening bat. Actually, do not use any form of *Wisden* on any of your own team. It may, however, be beneficial to the final result of the game if used on a trigger-happy umpire.

Play Running Late

Another curse of a cricket tea maker is a later than anticipated finish to an innings. This can be brought about by slow bowling or big hitting players clearing the sightscreens, causing mayhem on local roads and dislodging Rosemary tiles on the shopping centre roof. A cricket ball disappearing delivery after delivery is not a good sign for the tea maker's timing. An over-exuberant captain can also cause consternation in the clubhouse kitchen. These are captains who are following the ball as it disappears out of the ground (not actually onto the road as that's the job of the youngest member of the team) but rather placing a fielder where the ball has just been hit. This takes up crucial minutes.

They may, of course, have studied at the Captain Tinkerer's School of Minor Adjustment and are happy to move a fielder a centimetre to the left or right between each ball in an over. Such captains have no place in village cricket as they obviously have no responsibility or respect for the art and craft of a cricket tea and its maker. After all, rather like a cover drive, straight cut chips need to be timed to perfection. Taken out of the club's thermostatically wayward oven too early will

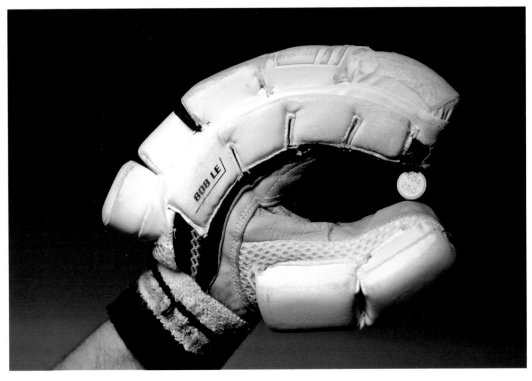

Indigestion – the ultimate disgrace of a cricket tea maker.

only result in an offering of a soggy mass of extruded potato mush. It will also culminate in a call from mid-on for a Gaviscon at around the three overs mark into the second innings.

This is in contrast to over-done chips. These can crack crowns, break bridges and fracture fillings. The call for an orthodontist is not one that a tea maker wants to hear while washing up on an otherwise peaceful Sunday afternoon in July. This whole area of irritation, suffered by so many novice tea makers, is easily soothed.

Either keep a watchful eye on the play while jamming up your bitesize scones or ask someone to report on the number of overs remaining, amount of wickets still to fall and which direction the dark clouds are moving. And consider asking the committee for money to fit a new thermostat to the club's oven.

Washing Up

Once the players are fed and watered and are waddling back out to resume play, it's only then that the terrifying spectre of the washing up emerges from the gently settling dust cloud of Pringles and Wotsits. Is the tea maker's job really done if there is a mountain of pots, pans and plates – scraped clean of course – to wash, dry and put away?

Well, no. Leaving crockery, grill pans and glasses unwashed is a mortal sin in the eyes of a true cricket tea maker. However, this is the time where non-skilled

A cricket tea maker's work is never done. Enlist help.

Clean plates should be stacked to ensure easy access for the next cricket tea maker.

members of the club can become involved. The ones who have absent-mindedly said 'if I can help, just shout' can indeed be shouted to. And then be shouted at. For it is a delicate job to distinguish between club budget feldspar and vintage wedding anniversary bone china items borrowed from the special sideboard at your parents' home.

The difference to an experienced tea maker is clear. Club crockery contains baked egg and detritus from 'sober-up breakfasts' no matter how many times it has passed through the dishwasher set to 'boil wash', whereas homeware is delicate, clean and, after one outing to the club, freshly chipped. But it can all be sorted and packed away. And then, and only when everything is shipshape and Bristol fashion, can the tea maker truly relax.

Emerging from the kitchen, drenched in sweat, ruddy cheeked and panting from the effects of dehydration, light deprivation and famine, the tea maker may get a chance to take in the final over of the game. However, the teams are usually already gearing up to hit the barbecue and are muttering about the whereabouts of the knives and forks and asking 'does this place ever have any tomato ketchup?' It's either that or the car park is already emptying. It's all in a day's play for the cricket tea maker.

Cricket Tea Maker: Team Dave

Clifton Alliance Cricket Club in York produces fantastic teas. A vibrant and friendly club, the current setup was formed after the merger in 1974 of Clifton Hospital Cricket Club and the Alliance Cricket Club. The teas are now served in a pavilion dating back to 1996 and both home and visiting players adore them. Those who watch like to tuck in as well. Dave Heartshorne is Club Chairman and tells his tea tale.

> We have to produce plenty of cricket teas during the season as we now have four adult teams, and they all need feeding at matches. It's a real committee and rota effort. Lots of people play a part in producing the teas because we felt that it was too much to expect one person to do them all. And new people coming in were slightly apprehensive about getting involved because of the good reputation of the teas. But now plenty help out and everyone mucks in.
>
> There's always plenty for players and supporters, who just put money into the donation pot if they take anything. It's better than actually pricing up items as some just want a bun and brew while others want a plateful. That's after the players have had theirs of course. It saves the tea makers from handling cash as well.

The quantity of food is vital to Dave and his team as these donations are essential for club funds, but quality is equally important.

Clifton Alliance
Cricket Club, York,
produce fantastic
cricket teas.

We like to keep it simple and uncomplicated. The most popular items are the usual meat, ham, cheese or chicken sandwiches. Younger players, especially in the third and fourth teams, like hot dogs and pizza, but knowing who is playing and what they might like is part of the success of a cricket tea.

We've started putting on a cheeseboard and players love it. It's also cheap and easy to do. I do like to buy as many different types of bread such as chilli-, olive- and onion bread, and cut them into chunks. When they are all put into baskets, it looks great and fills players up.

I reckon there's about twenty people involved in making the teas at the club. When fixtures have allowed it, we've even had the firsts and seconds making teas for the thirds. It's a great way of bringing the whole club together.

It's a real team effort which is lucky really as we do around forty teas a season. Cricket teas don't need to be a chore if you get everyone involved. Teas are also a way to show how proud you are of your club.

Cricket Tea Maker: And the Winner is …

I started going out with a cricketer when I was sixteen years old and I said to him from the start "if you think I'm going to watch cricket every weekend then you're wrong." I then started helping with the teas soon after. I became a regular and even now, sixty-three years after, I haven't had anyone come into the pavilion and say "that tea was horrible."

Vilma Buck (centre) with Charlotte Edwards CBE (left) and Beth Morgan (right), both former England internationals.

Vilma Buck encapsulates everything that cricket teas stands for. In Vilma, Worfield Cricket Club near Bridgnorth in Shropshire has an award-winning cricket tea maker of some repute. Awarded an Outstanding Service to Cricket Award (OSCA) by the Shropshire Cricket Board, Vilma has watched and fed teams her husband, son and grandson have played in. She has certainly seen some changes in her time as a cricket tea maker.

I remember setting out the long tables and having all the cricket teas pre-plated. We took the teas to the players as opposed to them using it as a buffet. You could also help yourself to whatever extras you could reach on the tables. The trick was not to sit with any gannets or you wouldn't get much.

Back then we all did homemade cakes and most of the ladies, and it was ladies back then, used to help. It was the only way we could all see our husbands. Nowadays, it has changed. The youngsters want things like Twix and Penguin biscuits and I wouldn't give you tuppence for cold pasta and cold rice. But you have to provide what the players want so that's what they get. Pizza and hotdogs are popular now.

I've recently done teas for Shropshire county age group matches and always like to put jelly and ice cream on as the boys and girls love that. I often get players coming into the pavilion before the game to ask if it's on the menu. The trick to a successful tea is to keep it as simple as you can and remember that players only have around twenty minutes' break to eat it.

Cricket Tea Maker: Raising the Bar

When you play at Uffington Cricket Club in Lincolnshire, you are in for a superb cricket tea. Dean Cornish, second eleven captain and master of running out his colleagues, explains why cricketers love their teas.

We're an enterprising bunch at Uffington Cricket Club and we've been striving to improve our club and the way we're perceived for years. The club has been in existence since 1858 and, up to recently, many opposition teams may have joked that some of the facilities hadn't been updated since then.

Up until 2014, our "pavilion" was an old mobile classroom borrowed from the local school. Making a decent tea in a shack with no electricity was nigh-on impossible. Some enterprising club members took it upon themselves to raise the funds for a new pavilion by numerous means, including a sponsored cycle to all English test venues over five days, as well as the more traditional village fete welly wanging and quiz night fundraisers. By the time 2014 had started, the club had a new pavilion and not only did that mean not having to change next to a lump of moss but, more importantly, a good, functioning kitchen was ours to make the best possible teas around.

When you play cricket, everyone knows the clubs where you get a good tea. We're lucky in the Rutland League as there are some cracking clubs around that

Uffington Cricket Club members play hard and fair to achieve high cricket tea points.

provide some superb teas. It's amazing how availability can swing from week to week, and it's never a surprise to the captains to see a full roster of players when you know there are cream scones on offer. Similarly, lots of players are strangely away with the kids when there's an away game in a none too salubrious area when you know you're only likely to be offered some takeaway pizza or even a plain bin bag full of rice (seriously – it happened to us!).

Knowing all this, we wanted to make sure that our teas were some of the best around. We wanted teams to enjoy coming to our place, and knew that offering a good tea was, let's face it, the number one reason. After all, they already knew they'd bowl us out for less than a hundred runs. We already rated opposition teas on the way home from each game, so we decided to do the same at home and start a home "tea of the year" competition. We weren't so lucky to have a regular "tea lady" so, with a rota of team players having to make tea, it was decided that the other players would give a mark out of ten for each tea and thus a secret score out of 100 was noted down next to the day's meagre bar takings.

At first it was a bit of fun but we were all amazed at how much the quality of the tea increased and how competitive it became. Lads who had never baked a cake in their life were suddenly enlisting their mums' help for lessons on how to do a Victoria sponge.

There were two rules to the competition. One was that every Uffington tea needed something you don't always get on a cricket tea. A cheese board would suffice certainly, as would some wonderful hot local sausages out of the oven, or even a range of samosas. Just something you don't get every week. Rule two was "no self-assembly." Too often at teas these days you get presented with loaves of bread, or a baguette and lots of open packets of ham, chicken and cheese slices.

Now, forgive me for being a cricket tea diva, but buttering one's own bread after forty-five overs in the field isn't for me.

Cricket is a superb sport, with so many fantastic nuances. For me, the English cricket tea is one of them.

Cricket Tea Maker: In the Balance

Annie Chave is the dedicated Secretary of The Erratics Cricket Club team in Exeter, Devon. Annie lives and breathes all things cricket.

My dad played for them back in the '70s and our weekends were always centred around the matches. I started scoring when I was nine years old and now both my husband and son play for the club. My dad's now the president. We did have a lovely home ground but twelve years ago that was sold, so now we are a nomadic team. All our matches are therefore played away and the cricket tea workload has gone from making teas every other weekend to us hosting around twelve teas a season at opposition grounds. We certainly relish those days and put a magnificent spread on.

The idea is that every player brings something to the match. Each player is designated a savoury, sweet or vegetarian item and, wherever we can, we use home

Annie Chave: cricket commentator, club secretary, passionate supporter of cricket and maker of tremendous cricket teas.

The Erratics Cricket Club, Exeter, play all matches away but still take pride in the teas.

produce. It's so different now from back in the day where I can remember long tables laid out with plates of food and I can still see the white cups and saucers with a green rim around the top.

Our cricket teas have always been buffet affairs and both quality and quantity are vital to a tea's success. For me, a homemade cake or two has to be in a tea and a great variety of sandwiches. As teams become more diverse, there is an increase in vegetarian items and obviously we enjoy catering for that.

Having made teas for years, my advice to anyone who is just starting to put their name on the cricket tea rota is to not leave all the preparation to the actual day of the match. Oh, and always keep an eye on the weather and of course the match itself.

A well-travelled member of The Erratics Cricket Club, Richard Hitchcock epitomizes what every cricketer feels about cricket teas.

My earliest cricket teas memory takes me back to the time when Mr Macmillan was Prime Minister, when 'you've never had it so good' and all was right with the world. That may have been true in the Home Counties, but not in rural Cornwall before the tourist boom. It was a wet Saturday in August – all Saturdays in August in Cornwall were wet in those days – but unless there was a consistent downpour cricket went on regardless.

The venue may have been Ladock Cricket Club, and we trooped off the field around 4 p.m. pretty well soaked to the skin, to be ushered into a barn with an earth floor and a corrugated iron roof, leaky where the rust had won. There we were each handed a mug of hot tea and a Cornish pasty, homemade to the traditional Cornish recipe of steak chunks, potato and swede. The balance of life was restored.

Armadillos CC
Sheffield Park
Sussex

◇◇◇◇◇

Armadillos Cricket Club in Sussex play at a picturesque
ground and produce the tastiest of teas.

Cricket Tea Maker: Into the Tail

Armadillos Cricket Club play at Sheffield Park in Sussex. It is a beautiful landscape immersed in history. It was in 1845 that cricket was first played at the ground. The opening bat for one of the teams was an Eton schoolboy, Viscount Pevensey. He later became Lord Sheffield, who not only inherited the ground, but became patron of both Sussex and England.

Matches involving India, South Africa and Australia in the late 1890s were played there, with crowds in excess of 25,000 marvelling at both the cricket and the scenery. During the Second World War, the garden, woods and buildings were split up and it wasn't until 2007, when the National Trust reunited the land and gardens, that cricket could be considered a viable opportunity. It was then that the Armadillos shuffled in. Extensive renovation of both the ground and pavilion soon created a sight to behold. And to taste. Johnny Colville, Honorary Secretary of the club, takes up the tea tale.

Cricket teas are the whole reason for the cricket games. The actual cricket is a secondary consideration. My wife's family includes a long line of chefs so seven trestle tables laden with sumptuous fare isn't a problem. There are usually acres of crusty scones, clotted cream and jam, every cake you can imagine, sandwiches with all the usual fillings, wooden skewers of strawberries, melon and grapes add a touch of fruit to the proceedings. A lot of Rocky Road is now being seen and the chocolate brownie competition to see who is heir to the brownie throne is getting more serious as the seasons go on.

Everyone brings something and you only get to play if you turn up with some goodies. The tower of cupcakes usually gets a lot of attention. We inevitably end up having two sittings. The first has to be the younger players and then the more senior players tuck in.

We have a lot of fun, the games are friendlies and all the sledging is between our players and never at the opposition. We do love cricket, and our teas, and play the "not out first ball" rule. Our honours board in the pavilion is remarkably untroubled but that doesn't matter. What does is everyone coming together. It's also a compliment that so many teams want to come and play us. I've no doubt that's testament to the standard of the scones and not the actual cricket.

But putting the scones to one side, why would anyone call a cricket club the 'Armadillos'? Johnny explains, 'It's quite apt really when you look at our cricket team. Armadillos are slow and steady with a long tail, gregarious and like to come out at night.'

Cricket Tea Maker: Mixing it Up

Slaughters Utd Cricket Club is nuzzled in the beautiful Gloucestershire countryside. Thanks to the efforts of Jo Shaw, Penny Hughes and a few friends, they have not only established senior men's sides but also junior sides and now a women's team is thriving at the club. Importantly, the cricket teas are sublime. Jo Shaw explains, 'My husband and son both play at the club so I used to help make teas at their games. But some of us felt that a women's team would be fun so we started one.'

Slaughters Utd Cricket Club in the Cotswolds have won prizes and many new members for their cricket teas.

Slaughters Utd were also part of The Great Cricket Tea Challenge in 2014 and after a gruelling judging process ended up winning the competition. 'It was great fun, slightly nerve wracking but a great experience.' But it's not just the men's matches that Jo and her friends cater for as the women's team is her priority.

> We do make the teas for the men but not all the time. Delegation is the key. The biggest difference between the men and the ladies' cricket teas is that for the ladies' team we tend to have less quantity but a better quality. The sorts of thing we have are strawberries dipped in chocolate, homemade Victoria sponge and coffee and walnut cake. Oh, and of course scones with whipped cream and jam.
>
> We aren't that great at cricket, but the teas are pretty good and, be it men's or ladies' teas, they are definitely the social part of cricket.

Cricket Tea Maker: Stellar Innings

Stella Deam is tea maker in chief at Avoncroft Cricket Club in Bromsgrove, Worcestershire. Every Saturday and Sunday in the cricket season, she creates spreads for the first and second teams. This kind of dedication is in many instances the only way a tea maker can see a partner or offspring at the weekend. But that's not the case with Stella.

Stella Deam is the mainstay of cricket teas at Avoncroft Cricket Club in Worcestershire, where umpires get special treatment.

Her husband occasionally pops down to the ground to help and her offspring aren't too fussed with the game so they don't see much of her from April until September. Stella started making the teas at Avoncroft Cricket Club six years ago after answering the plea for help from her brother-in-law. 'He asked me to help out so I did and I've being doing it ever since,' explains Stella.

My cheese and red onion sandwiches are a favourite and I put on all the usual such as ham, coronation chicken sandwiches, proper sausages, bowls of salads, chips and wedges, and I do buy in the cakes as I haven't got time to make homemade ones. But I don't offer scones.

The teams seem to love my teas. I tried putting fruit out for the first time this year and I noticed that it was the older players who enjoyed it most. The youngsters wanted the biscuits and cakes more.

I use paper plates for the players because it saves so much time on washing up, but I like to treat the umpires differently. They get proper china plates and cups and saucers, knives and forks and their own table. The scorers get the same and usually the scorers and umpires sit together. They always get to the tea first unless they say it is OK for the players to get stuck in. And everyone is always so appreciative and when they say thanks it makes it all worthwhile.

Cricket Tea Maker: Glam Tea

Southport & Birkdale Cricket Club in Lancashire is a super set-up with facilities only a few clubs can dream about. Often the venue for Lancashire CCC county games, the catering partners at the club not only feed first class players, officials and spectators, but teams at club level every week. Not that they are anything but first class as well of course.

Alan Green, third team Captain at the club, explains:

We put a lot of effort into encouraging the development side on a Sunday. It's a proper mix of young and experienced players and together they all learn. It's a great way to ensure the youth is developing through the club and beyond.

We also encourage the social side of cricket because it is so important to the overall game. That's why we provide a full Sunday roast for all the players, officials and spectators. We always tell the opposition that is the plan and one or two say that is a "bit heavy" especially if fielding second, but that's up to them. They can always say no and bring a few sandwiches or bowls of salad for themselves.

But we can get around fifty people tucking in alongside the players and that creates a special atmosphere. It brings in families as well and that can only be good for the club. We're lucky in that we have a superb caterer, Totally D'vine, making the roasts and that the scorers and umpires don't ask for payment. The cost of the meals comes out of the usual match subs.

Right: Southport & Birkdale Cricket Club, Southport, Lancashire, has superb facilities.

Below: A Glam Tea on a Sunday is just the job for hungry cricketers, friends and family.

Cricket Tea Maker: Sandwich vs. Victoria

Sandwich Town Cricket Club in Kent has a name synonymous with cricket teas. The club, established in 1823, is friendly, inclusive and set in the beautiful Garden of England and is keen on a super sarnie or two. Matt Van Poppel, First XI captain, tells their tea tales.

Teas take on extra significance at Sandwich Town due to the name and our tea ladies take their roles extremely seriously. We've even had competition with a local club, Deal Victoria, who were once voted the best teas in the country and invited to Lord's. Our tea ladies are rewarded for their efforts with a celebratory meal at the end of the season that is cooked and served by players and committee members.

This does mean that we also take it very seriously when the "conduct" of tea is not met at away grounds. It should always be the standard that the away team and officials are first in the line for tea and players are quick to suggest that I put the opposing club on my "blacklist" if this isn't the case.

Our tea ladies are always prepared for a few extra supporters and, on one occasion, this included a local homeless man who decided to join the queue and proceeded to try and convince everyone he was a player's dad when asked about it. One of our players felt sorry for him and went along with the story.

The Sandwich Town Cricket Club ladies ensuring that the club lives up to its name.

Michael Vaughan OBE believes that the lower the standard of cricket, the better the standard of tea.

My Favourite Cricket Tea

Michael Vaughan OBE, captain of the 2005 England Ashes winning side, scorer of thousands of runs in a long career, is now a respected and popular commentator on the game. He's someone who likes the crusts cut off his sandwiches at a cricket tea. How posh.

A cricket tea really should have sausage rolls, cakes, pork pies and sandwiches. And all different types of filling of course. I found at club level, when I was just starting out, that the lower the standard of cricket, the better the standard of cricket tea. Invariably made by the tea ladies of the club at quaint village grounds

Below: Michael on finding out that the crusts have been cut off the cricket tea sandwiches. It's that or he's celebrating a century for England against the West Indies in May 2007. (Photo: Simon Stacpoole/Offside)

in Derbyshire and Yorkshire, they didn't want to let the side down. They wanted their teas to be the talk of the town and never to be a disappointment. But crusts should always be cut off the sandwiches. That's the rule.

I can also remember chip butties being served between innings at some grounds and even when I became a professional, sandwiches and pies were still on the cricket tea table. Now, though, it's different. It's gone all scientific nonsense with energy bars and drinks. But when I started it was the captain's job to win the toss and bowl no matter what the conditions of the pitch were like. You bowled, tucked into the tea table and then, if you weren't opening, sat back and enjoyed the innings.

3

Putting the Ts in Tea-Takers

A towering innings.

Cricket is an all-inclusive sport, allowing every individual to play and compete in a team. And, when it comes to tea, all cricketers can be categorised as one of the following five types:

Stuffer

An interesting cricketer who gets full value from their match tax. He or she will always open the bowling, will bat in the top two, the ball will always find them on the field of play and at tea they will stuff food into their face while piling up a plate to tipping point.

They are also brazen about revisiting the tea table for a second and third helping. They are not averse to bucking the 'clockwise round the table only' rule to boldly dart against the run of play to get their greedy mitts on a gently steaming dollop of freshly cooked rice. They will also get a lift to and from the match.

Piler

Very much akin to the stuffer but without the stuffing. They have a modicum of social grace, are considerate to the fact that other players need to eat, but not enough to resist taking that final and, let's face it, lonely looking scone on the three-tiered display. A scone is a scone after all.

They do adhere to the 'one plate, one visit to the table' rule so are considered to be upper class by the stuffers.

Polite

Usually malnourished as they miss out on the bonanza of a highly crafted tea by allowing teammates to push in the queue, if there even is one, or generally allowing all and sundry to tuck in before they approach the table.

They consider themselves as being traditionalist whereas others call them hungry. They are happy with a quarter sandwich, a shattered Oreo and fragments of cheese and onion crisps. They have to be as the rest of the tea has long gone.

Wannabe Pro

Dreaded by tea makers around the village cricket circuit because Wannabes watch what they eat. They are the badgers of the cricket tea world in that they can recall the nutritional statistics for every item on a cricket tea table. They do not, like real badgers, eat worms, beetles and eggs of small birds. That would be way too calorific.

They have also been known to read the labels on packaging to ensure what they are eating is actually doing them an iota of good. Cricket clubs around the world tell tales of Wannabe Pros approaching tea makers asking for non-buttered brown bread with added seeds, enquiring about the whereabouts of the raspberry and nettle teabags and the availability of live unsweetened yoghurt. Quinoa is often their chosen topic as a conversation starter.

Their bodies are temples to fitness whereas 'stuffers' have bodies of special scientific interest. Wannabe Pros usually sit on their own at tea.

Sum total of a Wannabe Pro cricket tea. Hungry by 5 p.m.?

Bring Your Own, or BYO-ers

The cautious type who thinks too much about the origin of the teas. They have read reports on the state of hygiene in cricket pavilions and are in a perpetual panic over whether or not the tea maker on any given day owns cats and, if so, whether those

Taking your own cricket tea does remove any worries over the hygiene rating of homemade teas.

cats are allowed onto work surfaces. All perfectly reasonable thoughts but they do tend to miss out on the gratification of flossing a hard to reach molar with a twangy ginger strand of feline fur ingested from a ladle of congealed pasta topped off with a wedge of Victoria sponge, a handful of chips and four ham sandwiches.

It's a lifestyle choice and not one that every cricketer chooses.

Cricket Tea Taker: Mark Marks

Ashes clashes are usually memorable and the third test in the series at Trent Bridge, Nottingham, in July 1985 was no exception.

David Gower played at his elegant best in the first innings, scoring a majestic 166, with Mike Gatting and local boy Tim Robinson chipping in with half centuries plus. The Australians also enjoyed the batting conditions with Greg Ritchie and Graeme Wood amassing over 300 runs between them in one innings.

But ten miles away a seventeen year old was opening the batting for his local village side, Papplewick and Linby Cricket Club, in an away fixture at Sutton Bonington Cricket Club. Mark Birkin has always been immersed in cricket but on that day his head was turned. Not by Gower, whose bat Mark already replicated, or indeed Robinson's patient approach to batting or even by the gritty determination of the Australians, but by a special tea. A cricket tea he had never experienced before and hasn't since that fateful day.

> I don't actually remember how many runs I scored, that's if I scored any of course, or even the result of our match, but what I do remember is the cricket tea. It's the one I always use as a benchmark and, to be honest, even after all the years I've

Papplewick and Linby Cricket Club in Nottinghamshire, home to quality cricket and superb teas.

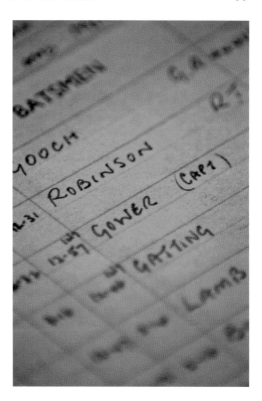

David Gower OBE played sublimely
at Trent Bridge, Nottingham, in 1985,
keeping the scorer busy for hours.
Tea was taken on time.

played cricket, none has ever surpassed it. A couple of friends in the team and I always scored the teas and wrote the results in a book. The book has long gone now but the memories of that tea remain.

I'd never had a sit down tea at cricket before so it was quite a moment to be seated and presented with plates of sliced meats, a plate of salad and homemade cakes. Remember, I was an impressionable seventeen years old.

All the teas we had during the seasons got marks for quantity, quality, choice and if any of the items were homemade then that scored them even higher. This one had the lot. There were even condiments, real plates as opposed to disposable ones and cakes on cake stands. The tea was served in proper china cups. It was everything you imagined a cricket tea to be and it was definitely a taste of Utopia. After all, cricket teas are a cricketing tradition.

Cricket Tea Taker: The Dog Who Came to Tea

It's not always the players and officials who scoff the contents of a cricket tea. Sometimes, despite a solid defence, wickets fall. Glynis Culley (née Hullah) is a former England women's international who made her debut at Old Trafford against Australia in 1976 and has a tale to tell.

Glynis Culley,
England
international in
the 1970s.

It's not one from her four test appearances or twenty ODIs. This one harks back
to village cricket in Great Missenden in Buckinghamshire.

The Great Missenden team did not play league cricket, just friendly games either
on a Saturday or Sunday. My husband John's best pal Richard was captain of the
team. There was a tea rota for each home match. Sometimes a wife, mother or
girlfriend was persuaded to help but it was not unusual for the players themselves
to prepare the tea and set it out in the pavilion ready for the interval.

On this particular Saturday it was Richard's turn to prepare tea. Unfortunately
there was a lack of help so Richard set the tea out, covered in clingfilm and foil,
ready for the break as Great Missenden were fielding.

Now, Richard had a beloved Labrador called Mollie. Mollie rarely went on a
lead and was usually seen at Richard's heel. Mollie was cricket trained. She knew
she was not to step over the boundary line while Richard was fielding or batting so
usually lay patiently in wait until Richard returned.

As we know, Labradors are renowned for gluttony. They would eat themselves
to death given a chance and Mollie nearly did that. She snuck into the pavilion
and started to lay into as much food as she could. It was only when a player went

Guilty as charged.

in to turn on the urn that the carnage was uncovered. The tea was decimated. Sadly, there was nothing left to eat that had not been half chewed or eaten by the lovely Mollie.

Fortunately, the opposition saw the funny side of events and Mollie, well I doubt she needed to eat for a week plus she was definitely in the doghouse.

Cricket Tea Taker: Taking the Strain

A cricket tea obviously includes sandwiches, cake and the like, but also that essential cup of tea, generally brewed and stewed in metal silos that haven't been cleaned for decades. The general argument for never cleaning out the cavernous vessel is that the coating of tannin actually adds to the flavour of the resultant brew.

Patrick Latham recounts a horror story that the people involved, the players, don't know about. Until now that is. Names of the tea lady and the teams involved have been deleted to protect the innocent. But not Patrick's so you may be able to work out whether or not you were there.

The sorry tale begins at the start of a season a few years ago. At a ground in the Midlands.

The industrial-sized tea pot the tea lady used to slosh in the general direction of a collection of mugs wasn't pouring quite as freely as it was at the end of last

Left: Patrick Latham spills the beans.

Below: A tasty brew with added protein.

season. Tea was being sprayed all over the work top and was starting to seep into the carpet.

The tea lady in question still hadn't worked out how many tea bags were required in the vessel. That appeared to be a club secret.

The cricket tea was served and the players trudged out of the pavilion, duly fed and watered. As she was washing up the reason for the troublesome tea pot suddenly became clear. Twenty-two cricketers and four officials had just seen off three gallons of tea, all strained through a dead mouse that, over the winter, had fallen into the tea pot. The mouse had tried climbing up the spout in a vain effort to escape only to become lodged there, where it had passed away over four months previously. The mouse slithered back down the spout and nestled among the used teabags in the bottom of the pot.

The tea lady quietly disposed of the soggy little carcass in the bin. As she walked past the opposition players they all enthusiastically thanked her again for her efforts with the teas.

Cricket Tea Takers: Scorers' Tales

Whether it's a skein, stand or scurry, the scorers know the score. Just as players and umpires judge a tea, the people who facilitate a result of any sort are not far behind once they have totted up the bowling analysis and cross-checked totals with each other.

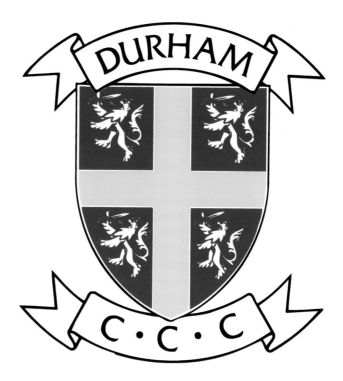

Durham scorers know where the best cricket teas are.

Scorers have to be honest and meticulous. Keith Telford, Peter Connolly and Jack McGurk are experienced scorers from Durham and fit the bill to perfection. They have the privilege of visiting many grounds around the country to sample the varying standards of cricket, musty score boxes and, of course, the local hospitality.

They are all appreciative of the teas and there is general agreement that where provided by volunteers they are usually better than outside caterers. But what do these particular specialists in a cricket match enjoy seeing on a tea table?

'Depends on the day, but I do prefer a hot meal and of course a good cup of tea. We get carried away with this nutrition aspect. After a day in the field or in the score box it is good to get a variety of food – even a salad can be appreciated but not too often,' says Keith. Cake is usually big in every cricketer's and cricket official's life, and it's no different for the well-travelled Durham scorers. Keith's favourite is 'a cream scone with a strawberry on top. That can always be relied upon at Manor Park in Norwich.' 'The best cricket teas I've ever, ever had were at Darlington Cricket Club when Mrs Mulholland was responsible for their production,' recalls Peter.

But here the scorebooks don't tally. Jack says, 'Hartlepool Cricket Club, on County Second XI or Under 17s days are the best teas you could imagine.'

A discrepancy? Perhaps the collective noun for scorers is actually a squabble? Start again from the first ball and rebuild.

When it comes to county grounds Peter says, 'I think Grace Road takes some beating when it comes to catering. And Durham of course.'

However, cricket tea makers should take note as there are some items that the scorers do not want to see on the trestle tables. Peter warns, 'Deep fried chicken drumsticks should not be part of a cricket tea as they make your fingers all greasy.' And no one wants a slippery pen or fingerprints on the scoresheet.

Other items that should not be presented to the Durham scorers' collective are, according to Jack, 'watery chilli and/or curry on the tea table with no other choice.'

Jack is also slightly controversial in his diet. He doesn't eat much cake but 'could however be tempted by the strawberry sponge or profiteroles on the Hartlepool tea table.' It's understandable.

Cricket Tea Taker: Press

Kevin Howells is the unmistakable voice of county cricket. He's seen more county cricket matches than he's had hot dinners and firmly believes that the cricket tea is fundamental to the bigger game.

I've never played "proper" cricket but we did develop a social side when I was at BBC Radio Shropshire. But my love of the game blossomed when I moved to BBC Radio Leeds where one of my jobs was to follow and report on Yorkshire CCC.

I started covering the second XI matches where the teas were fantastic at grounds such as Todmorden, Stamford Bridge and Elland. I've been lucky to visit all the county grounds and cricket festivals, with Scarborough being one of the best.

Kevin Howells is the voice of county cricket – when he isn't missing the action and placing the blame on fruit cake.

On one occasion, the cricket tea was laid out in the marquee and quite rightly all the dignitaries were first in the queue. The media had to wait. Unfortunately, by the time we had finished tucking in the actual game had re-started and a few wickets had fallen. But what's more important at a Scarborough festival – the cricket or the food? Obviously the food on that occasion.

And on the county circuit Kevin looks forward to certain items being on the tea table. 'Pizza and hotdogs are I suppose a bit modern, but chips are always welcome. And sausage rolls, scones of course and fruit cake is a must.' As any cricket tea maker knows, it takes a lot of time, effort, skill and determination to create a cricket tea, so why bother going to a lot of effort when a few prepacked sandwiches and cakes would suffice?

If you keep the crowd and players happy then they will come back. Well-fed commentators may well be swayed to say nice things about the team. It's not bribery of course. It's also right that members are proud of their club. There's no better way to show off that pride than with a proper cricket tea.

Cricket Tea Taker: Delia, Where are You?

Over thirty years ago, Stephen Chalke played for a touring team at a village called Battisford in Suffolk.

I was the team's fixture secretary, and my opposite number was a chap called Mike Wynn-Jones. When we came off for tea, we had to walk down this long trestle table

Stephen Chalke encountered
Delia Smith without knowing
it. Or did he?

where there were all these home-baked cakes, with a different woman hovering
over each one, almost defying you to walk past without taking a slice of their cake.
I ended up with a plate stacked high with cake slices, earning myself the nickname
of Bunter for the rest of the day.

You could really sense the competitiveness between all these women with their
cakes. I've never forgotten it. Only three or four years ago I was reading a feature
in the newspaper, and I discovered that Mike Wynn-Jones was the husband of
Delia Smith, who could well have been among the women there. Immediately this
strange scene in my memory became clear.

Cricket Tea Taker: What a Jaffa

It was natural evolution to move from playing at club level to umpiring, and John
Russell did it with relish. Officiating in leagues in both Scotland and England, it was
in Aldershot in Hampshire where he most fondly remembers the cricket teas.

I was umpiring the Army cricket team and, when it came to tea, we all marched
off the playing area and into tents to enjoy the most memorable of teas. They were

John Russell, former league cricket umpire, loves a well-ordered British Army cricket tea.

always prepared by the Army Catering Corps and they quite enjoyed showing off their prowess at making teas. The teas were always lavish and much appreciated by the umpires and most of the players.

I say "most" because during one particular tea interval, the highly entertaining banter between the players turned to the story of mounds of sausages and mash that had been served up only a few days before. It was cold on that particular day and, seeing that the players were shivering, the caterer decided everyone needed something hot. I'm sure some soldiers would have that no matter what the weather was.

On the day I was umpiring, it was slightly warmer so magnificent salads, meats and vegetables were all expertly prepared and served. At the end of the tea table there was a large bowl of fresh fruit and everyone dipped in. We went back onto the field of play to resume the match.

I took the bowler's sweater and gave him the ball. He paced out his run up, the batsman settled and I called "play". He charged in and bowled a full toss at the

'Bowling a Jaffa' may have its origins at Aldershot in the late 1990s.

batsman who promptly connected juicily with the ball. Or orange, a Jaffa orange to be precise, substituted by the bowler for the ball. Bits flew everywhere.

They were great games, full of good-hearted humour and a terrific standard of hard but fair cricket. Everything you would expect from a British Army team. And the teas weren't too bad either.

Cricket Tea Taker: Cow Corner

Chris Walsh is midweek skipper at Fleckney Village Cricket Club in Leicestershire. Chris has played for over twenty-five years and is an experienced cricket tea taker.

My earliest memory of Sunday cricket tea was when I played at Tilton & Lowesby in Leicestershire. The match was played next to the grand Lowesby Hall in a cow field – you had to drive through the field to find it. Tea was two pasting tables covered in full-size, homemade cakes and sandwiches. I was troughing for hours (I was thirteen).

The next away match was a similar cow field at Ridlington in Rutland. Tea was taken after the match, which we won by one wicket chasing twenty-one all out. To get to the tea in the village hall, we were led through the captain's house. Not his garden, his actual house! His wife sat completely oblivious to our presence watching TV as we marched through.

One tea I always look forward to is at Old Cricket Club, a village in Northamptonshire. At tea time, they simply lock the pavilion and head to the pub. Another Northants teatime treat can be found at Bugbrooke Cricket Club. There was a delay at tea once as they hadn't finished putting the cream on the scones.

Leicester Market Traders Cricket Club used to put on a fantastic spread. Obviously they had the pick of the fresh produce. I remember complimenting them on a tea and how good it was and they said it was poor by their standards. It was their reserve tea lady. We are lucky to even have one.

On tour, we once travelled to Selling Cricket Club in Kent. The tea they served up literally contained everything. Sandwiches, wraps, pork pies, scotch eggs, hot dogs, burgers, every fruit you have ever heard of including starfruit.

But not all teas are good. Due to the fact we keep getting relegated, we now play a lot of park cricket clubs from the old inner-city Leicester mutual leagues. There's obviously nothing wrong with the cricket; it's just that having a kitchen is not in the ground's criteria.

One club served us tea in an old shipping container during a thunderstorm. We ran for the car. Another side walked into our changing room and handed us just two trays of cheese sandwiches (red Leicester as well – not even the nicest cheese in Leicester. No one here likes luminous cheese)

Chris Walsh, stalwart of Fleckney Village Cricket Club, on hearing that custard creams are absent from the day's cricket tea.

The worst though had to be playing on Western Park where, with no changing room or outside furniture, at the break the opposition threw four cold pizza boxes on the floor and left us to it.

One club which actually delivered us a good tea charged us the exact sum of £38.70. It was a team of teachers – perhaps maths or accountancy?

My Favourite Cricket Tea

Jack Simmons MBE is the embodiment of a cricketing legend. He achieved his first class debut for his home county of Lancashire aged twenty-seven; he helped the county win numerous One Day titles in the 1970s; and, in a career spanning over twenty years, he took over 1,000 first class wickets with his right arm off break bowling and scored over 9,000 runs.

Jack's bowling style, or the trajectory of the ball, was perfect for one day competition and earned him one of his nicknames, 'Flat Jack'. Mention his name to any avid cricket fan and eyes will mist over and personal memories of the great man will start to flow. He is also known for his appetite.

When I was playing in the Lancashire League, we just got a sandwich. I cannot remember getting anything else, maybe an occasional sausage roll, or a meat pie. When I went to Blackpool on a Sunday for extra practice, you sat down to a knife and fork salad. I can always remember thinking this is posh, but very nice. And as you will have noticed, I am not a big salad eater.

County cricket teas were very much the same, except getting a big salver of mixed sandwiches, with occasionally fruit cakes. Lords always seemed to be the best for lunches and teas, but there wasn't a great deal of difference between the counties for teas. I would have loved seeing a meat pie or sausage roll, or a hot dog or a pizza. You would have had a mad rush off the field, in my day, or even in the dressing room for that kind of tea. I was always pleased when we got a meat pie, but that was only in league cricket. They wouldn't dare to put them on at Lancs.

I always enjoyed cheese and tomato sandwiches with a good cup of tea and my favourite cakes are still jam sponge and carrot cake.

Lancashire Cricket

Jack Simmons, Lancashire County Cricket Club, on debut at Blackpool in 1968.

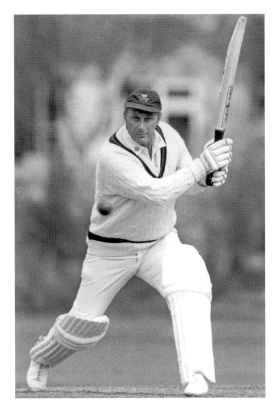

Left: Best known for his bowling, 'Flat Jack' was useful with the bat. (Credit: Mark Leech)

Below: Jack Simmons MBE is a true legend of the game.

4

Putting the T in Favourites

Every cricketer has their favourite cricket tea table treat. But too much of a good thing can lead to taste buds becoming jaded. Variety is the key to a happy season and a long and successful cricketing career.

The cricket tea maker can ensure a rich tapestry of offerings by carefully considering the vitally important savoury:sweet ratio. It's true to say most cricketers love a cake or three, but only when counterbalanced by a savoury offering along the lines of pesto pasta or a serving spoon overflowing with boiled, lightly buttered new potatoes. A tea table laden with sweet sacrifices certainly gets the juices flowing but is it really the ideal scenario? No.

After extensive and, to protect the innocent, anonymous research into cricket tea peccadillos (not to be confused with a hard Italian cheese made from sheep's milk) it is true to say that the ideal savoury:sweet ratio is 3:1.

In addition, the ideal overall colour of a cricket tea when viewed from the pavilion doors is rainbow. Or at least a little splash of green in among the vanilla. Do remember as a cricket tea maker that though the sentiment of green is a good thing, take-up will be low. You have tried your best and that is all any club can ask.

Once your ratio is correct and a healthy vitamin packed addition has been made to your tea, rest assured all items will be heaved onto one plate by each and every team member. Therefore, it can be quoted with extreme confidence that the favourite item on a cricket player's plate is:

VictoriaspongecoffeecakecarrotcakeflapjacksconescoconutcakeplainspongeBlack ForestgateaucheeecakesinanyflavourbanoffeepiecrèmebruleetrifleEtonmesscarrot scucumberslicesbeetroottotestthecleaningclaimsofmostpowdersangelcakemering ueincludinglemonraspberryandwhitechocolatebabkabatikavocadofruitofcoursefr uitcakeisincludedwithslicesofcheeseifplayinginDerbyshireorpartsofYorkshireparki nsimnelforearlyseasongamesateasterbarabrithwiththankstoGlamorganbrowniesin anyshapeorsizegoodoldfashionedchocolatecornflakesandchocolatekrispiescupcak

Hitting a delivery with the main ingredient of a cricket tea crumble is a skill way above anything else. Not many people achieve this feat; just one in fact.

esofcoursecupcakesEcclescakesandChorleycakeswheninLancashirenotPontefractc
akesastheyaresweetssurelyGenoa(yesIdo)Lamingtoncakeorangeandpolentacakeredv
elvetcakerumcakebutgoeasyontheessentialingredientifopeningthebattingStrawberry
cakesandsandwicheswithanyfillingorwrapsforthemoreadventurousSwissrollArcticro
lltarttatinappleandcaramelcakeanythingwithsaltedcaramelincludedisalwayswelcome
moresandwichesupsidedowncakeorbacktofrontcakeifthethermostatintheovenisplayi
nguplikeadodgyscoreboardlightsausagerollsCornishpastiesrockcakeschocolaterolls
wrappedinsilverorpurplefoilanybiscuitswrappedinfoilfromavarietytinBakewellpudd
ingsandtartspestopastanewpotatoesdrippinginrealbutterornewpotatoesdrippingin
margarineornewpotatoesdrippingindrippingoutofdatehalloweencakesmadebyMrK
iplingbuttheyweregoingcheapandfitnicelyintothebudgetsoletsusethemandnooneactu
allytasteswhattheyeatanywaymuffinsareagoodwaytopretendtotakeonboardfruitespe
ciallyblueberriesmarblecakelemondrizzlebuttheicinghastobeeversoslightlycrunchyla
yercakejaffacakesoraretheybiscuits(theyarecakes)butwhocaresastheyarejaffacakesa
ndthereforehavetobeonacricketteatablechocolatefingersbourboncreamscustardcrea
msjammiedodgerssheetsofgaribaldidigestiveschocolatedigestiveshobnobspenguinb
iscuitsandcheaperalternativesmarketedaroundotherlessamusinganimalsfreddosshor
tbreadgingernutswagonwheelsfigrollsforolderteamsandonlyiftheyhavefieldmaltedm
ilk(ditto)tryandgetsportsbiscuitsforthecricketstickmankitkatstunnockswafersmary
landcookiesandthepacketsoftheminiversionofthesamefatrascals(butthatisthirdmani
nmostteams)macaroonsfairingsmueslibarsfortheyoungkeenmembersoftheteamLinc
olnbiscuitsClubbiscuitsandhopeforathickendofchocolatebutnotthemintflavouredo
nesdogbiscuitsforthecirclinganimalsandgroundstaffmincepiesandbrandybutterTim
TamsforAustralianplayerstofeelathomeifnotactuallyathomeFlorentinebiscuitsfora
nyItalianplayersoranyonewhocanprounouncegnocchicorrectlygnocchiMarieNice
(allbiscuitsarenice)partyringsShrewsburycakeforminorcountyplayersinthewest
VienessewhirlsbrandysnapsforloucheplayersinLondonarrowrootbiscuitsAfghanbis
cuitforanyKiwisorAfghansandfinallyarichteaorfivefortheumpiretodunk.Itshouldbe
sixbutsomeumpiresscorersandbowlersoftenstruggletoagreeonthatnotablefigure.

Cricket Tea Takers' Favourites

'This is the kind of tea we want. No thrills. Just simple tucker. Lovely.' What a thrilling way to hear that your tea has hit that sweet spot. 'They were the words of the late, great Tony Catley, stalwart of Exning CC, singing our praises,' explains Huw Turbervill, President of Woodbridge Cricket Club (formerly Deben Valley Cricket Club).

Yet again I and my loyal deputy Ed Parker at Deben Valley CC had been pressed into action that morning in the mid-1990s, the lack of volunteers forcing us into a hungover trip to the Co-Op. Rolls. Cheese. Ham. Cheese and ham. Crisps. A few cakes. Teabags. Unlikely to set the pulses racing on *The Great British Bake Off*, I agree. But as Mr Catley said, it did the job.

Huw Turbervill (right), Woodbridge Cricket Club, chatting to former England international Chris Tavaré about the merits, or otherwise, of cucumber in a cricket tea.

And Huw has played cricket for almost four decades and has firm ideas on what should and should not be in a cricket tea.

No cucumber. It gives you indigestion. Wait for the visitors to go first. Manners maketh man (and woman) and don't eat too much if you are opening the bowling after tea. But most importantly, it's a great tradition – don't let it die!

Cricket Tea Takers' Favourites

Some players do have particular favourite memories from particular grounds, but sometimes it's only the food that sticks around. Sam Fletcher at Papplewick and Linby Cricket Club in Nottinghamshire fondly remembers 'Hot dogs and doughnuts at Goosedale, Nottinghamshire, and bread and dripping somewhere up North.' Other favourites from club cricketers include pie, chips, peas and gravy at Fleetwood Cricket Club; corned beef sandwiches anywhere; Marmite sandwiches and only Marmite sandwiches; mini gingerbread men and one player insisting on only eating cheese and coleslaw sandwiches. Angie Broughton, who creates marvellous cricket teas at Kibworth in Leicestershire, has clear views on what needs to be on a cricket tea table.

Cricketers do like Battenberg, Bakewell's, chocolate cake (any sort), carrot cake, well, any cake really. They are creatures of habit. They don't like anything to change. The lot I do teas for don't really like salad, whether it's in a sandwich or in a bowl. The younger teams like hummus but the older teams won't go near it.

Euan Woods scoring 142 for Surrey County Cricket Club Under 17s at Arundel and it's down to a quality cricket tea. And other factors such as skill and training, of course.

> I normally do seven different fillings of sandwiches. Cake, pizza, pasta, crisps and fruit. All served with mugs of tea.

Keith Greenfield, Director of Cricket at Sussex CCC, scored more than 7,000 runs for the county and has represented Sussex at all levels of the game. Now, as Director of Cricket, he still reminisces about the grounds where he enjoyed cricket teas. Arundel Castle, Preston Nomads and Three Bridges Cricket Club are all stand out grounds for teas where scones, jam and clotted cream and pork pies all feature. Like so many other cricketers, Keith is a fan of carrot cake.

Euan Woods is a useful all-rounder and has played for Surrey at U15s, U17s, Surrey CCC 2nd team, Hampshire 2nds as well as England U19s. According to his mum, Michelle, 'He can be quite fussy but I think cricket food has actually made him a better eater as he realised it was what was on offer or nothing and go hungry.'

Euan plays in the Home Counties Premier League on Saturdays and his team, Henley Cricket Club, have some fabulous teas including Thai green curries, fajitas with all the trimmings, jacket potatoes filled with beans, cheese, tuna or chilli. Then at the other end of the 'was that a great cricket tea or what?' scale there are clubs that always serve lasagne and sausage and chips. A little bit on the heavy side for this particular left-handed batsman and right-handed off spinner.

Another up and coming star of the future is Ethan Bamber, England U19s, Middlesex second eleven and fan of tea maker Yvette's North Middlesex Cricket Club teas. Especially the cookies. 'Yvette's teas are the best and a nice chocolate or peanut butter cookie at tea always goes down a treat,' admits Ethan.

Ethan Bamber's cookie intake is vital to his success at Middlesex County Cricket Club.

My Favourite Cricket Tea

The Yorkshire Diamonds are a formidable force in women's T20 cricket. Formed in 2016, the squad boasts a deep pool of talent and it's Jane Hildreth's job as general manager to organise the team.

Jane is well placed to be adept at all things cricket having been brought up with the sport from an early age: 'My dad played for Wighill Park Cricket Club in Yorkshire, a club steeped in tradition.' It is the club where Lord Hawke, a cricketing colossus, once played and who is often referred to as the father of Yorkshire cricket. 'I was always around the cricket because dad played and mum did the teas. Once I got married, the only way I could see my husband in summer weekends was by doing the teas at his matches.'

And now Jane is looking after the Yorkshire Diamonds and her responsibilities includes the team's nutrition.

We have strict ECB guidelines on nutrition and that's a great support to us and all cricket teams. The players love it. Being the T20 format, we have food at the beginning of the game and after it has been completed. High protein foods are perfect before an innings and that includes warm chicken, fish, salads, fruit, nuts and yoghurt. After a game many of the players have long journeys so that's the perfect time for lasagne, chilli, rice and muffins.

We sometimes have a BBQ after a game and any meat is lean. Of course the occasional cake is allowed, it's up to the girls, but they know the level of commitment to fitness that's required of top class players these days.

It sounds a far cry from cake-laden tea tables at village clubs, but as Jane explains, 'The correct nutrition is essential in helping the players perform to their best. And it goes beyond match days.'

Above: Yorkshire Diamonds take a scientific approach to nutrition.

Right: Jane Hildreth, General Manager of Yorkshire Diamonds, is key to the success of the team.

5

Putting the Ts in Etiquette

Biscuits stacked
Jenga-style by the
opposition = target for
hostile bowling. It's just
how it is.

The etiquette of a traditional village cricket tea is a dichotomous mix of greed and courtesy. Of course the ravenous opener who has just carried his bat for twenty-seven hard-fought runs against 'some of the best bowling this side of the post office' should be offered first pickings at the spread, but equally the first-choice bowler who is about to ply his trade needs to fuel up for his potentially devastating and local newsworthy opening spell of two overs from the dog-chew factory end.

And then of course there are the officials. Two umpires and a couple of scorers need sustenance to ensure full concentration. At tea, they still have three more hours of synapse-scorching decisions and the deliberate selection and correct use of coloured pens.

Cricket tea etiquette needs to be sustained for future generations. Here's how:

Pre-Tea Snaffling

Nobody likes the pre-tea snaffler (PTS.) These could be the players who have batted and are out combined with those who have still to bat. All are feeling peckish. In other words, 9 /11ths of one side. They are hovering around the tea table watching as the spread develops. For some reason they feel that a crafty sausage roll or pilfered handful of jelly snakes is theirs to be taken. No, no, no. The only way to stop PTSers is to guard the tea table. There are several ways to do this.

Simply covering the fare with clingfilm is not good enough. Firstly, PTSers can see what's on offer and this is often too tempting for most lower order batsmen. Secondly, clingfilm never actually clings to food or the plates. It is exceptional at cloying to your hands, your jumper and the bin lid. Foil is a better alternative as it has the added benefit of making noise when disturbed. A little bit like the umpires.

One glare from the groundsman will keep the cricket tea table safe.

A secondary form of PTSer you have to guard against is the club groundsman who feels that because he has spent all morning preparing a wicket for a team he isn't even selected for, he is deserved of a slice of quiche or rock cake before everyone else. In fact, thinking about it, he or she probably is.

Put the groundsman's ability to clear a herd of All Stars young cricketers off a glaringly obviously roped-off cricket square with one glower to good use. No one takes on the groundsman and survives to tell the tale. Just ask the under 15s who once used the decrepit covers as a cloak of faux-invisibility when experiencing their first lungfuls of tobacco. If only they were still at the club.

Also, it's important to remember that you can utilise an appeasing cake for the greater good of the wider tea. That ancient saying 'A sacrificial scone goes a long way in preserving the Battenberg' springs to mind. That's a lesson in life and should be on every cricket badge and preferably in Latin for added authority: 'A vadit sacrificatum scone longo itinere simulacrumque servare Battenburg'.

Patrol

You can patrol the tea table once it is set. Depending on how long the table is, this may require motion sickness tablets. It will definitely require eyes in the back of your head. It is worth considering that as you patrol you are advertising a spread worthy of attention. And when you need to open the oven door to release the build-up of moisture to prevent your basic value margarita pizza from steaming as opposed to baking, there may be attacks.

Once the spread is complete, it is much safer to clear the pavilion of cricket stragglers and superfluous players, lock the pavilion doors, close any blinds and turn off all lights. A head torch will be useful if the oven light isn't working.

A trusted colleague can relay the state of play and any incoming weather likely to alter the timing of tea by a predetermined system of knocks on the bolted door.

Umpires First

It is traditional that umpires get first dibs at the tea. You may think that because they've been relatively immobile for three hours they are not entitled to first choice. You are wrong on two counts.

When watched carefully through the gap in the curtains (while locked in the pavilion guarding the Jaffa Cakes and Mini Rolls), you will note they walk a few metres every five minutes. Exhausting work.

Secondly, and more importantly, never forget that umpires potentially hold the outcome of the match in their hands. Or on their fingers. Or on one finger. The index finger. Treat them well and they will feel good towards your team. Invite the officials in, offer up the full, unsullied spread and the marginal 'surely that's knocking off pole out of the ground Ump?' query goes in your favour, the decision swayed by the warmth of a sausage roll straight from the oven.

It isn't bribery, merely a process called 'nudging'. Governments and big businesses use the technique all the time, albeit not usually with hot pastries. You may hear cricket commentators describing a particular batter as a good 'nudger'. You now know why.

Let umpires go first at tea time – they may be exhausted after carrying a lot of paraphernalia for hours.

Treat the umpires well and that LBW shout may go in your favour. Cheating? No. Nudging? Yes.

Home Team

When you are the home team you know in your heart that it is a case of allowing the opposition to approach the tea table after the officials. It's often a difficult etiquette guideline to swallow but a general courtesy nonetheless.

If you had guests at your house you wouldn't announce that dinner is served and then elbow them out of the way, rushing to the mushroom vol-au-vents and being first to glug directly from the bottle of Blue Nun? Of course not. Allow the opposition to tuck into the tea, obviously doing the polite thing and offering them the small side plates and then closely monitor who is stacking up the chocolate fingers in a Jenga-style fashion. That person then becomes a fair target for hostile bowling. Obviously.

Watch the opposition captain at all times as any eyebrow movement or twitch of the head is a sign for you and your plague of locusts to descend. Top class sides can also detect any previous night's drinking session induced, trapped-nerve flickering eyelid in the home team captain. Be warned.

Captain's Call

There are times when the opposition team captain will usher you and your team into the tea melee before his own crew. This is usually when the captain is shiny,

Crushed cherry Bakewells can double up as an effective thigh pad. Remove foil cases before use to avoid unnecessary chafing.

keen and in need of a post-innings chat with a few of his players. His players do not usually go along with this tactic.

Do, however, take advantage of this act of generosity, finding the large dustbin-sized plates squirrelled away behind the bar and for use by home team players only. Or take the lids off the actual dustbins and any metal incinerators and use them.

Fill pockets to bursting capacity with cherry Bakewells. No one will dare target you and your audacity with their hostile bowling. And if they did, rest assured that three compacted cakes are as effective as any top grade thigh pad. Remember to remove any foil cases to avoid the risk of chafing.

Social

It would be nice to think that opposing teams can sit together at tea, discuss the innings, state of the pitch, perhaps the prevailing weather and laugh about the inept decisions of the umpires (currently last in the queue for the tea and anxiously watching as the hand-crimped mini-pasties are loaded onto the satellite dish of a plate held by the home team's specialist short leg; or 'hollow legs' to be more accurate). It would be nice but not many teams actually do it. There may be some social interaction between tobacco smokers outside on the pavilion steps, but that never lasts long, unless players are related. In some parts of the country, this is the entire team.

Anti-social behaviour can be avoided by having a sit down tea table with name cards. Announce this to players entering the pavilion as 'We are doing things differently here from now on. It's home team player, away team player, home team player, away team player and everyone moves around after the pasta course. Enjoy.' It's one way to ensure you will never be asked to do the teas again. Especially saying 'enjoy'. That and handing the umpires shield-sized plates while creating a human block to marauding players.

Plates

Whatever size of plate you choose or are given, it needs to be emptied. Leave one crumb of a lightly masticated chocolate chip cookie and the day's tea maker will be distraught, demanding reasons why it wasn't good enough and possibly having a nervous breakdown in front of your eyes. Plates and glasses will be thrown with great gusto. Even if it means surreptitiously feeding one of the many and varied dogs found circulating beneath every cricket tea table, clear your plate.

And then take that empty plate to the chief washer-upper and thank whoever is around for a wonderful tea. It doesn't matter who you thank, just do it loud and proud. 'Thank you ladies' is now considered sexist. Boys makes teas as well, you know. You will generally find that boy washing up.

Always clear your plate to avoid insulting the tea maker. Wear safety glasses if returning a plate containing food.

Post-Tea Filcher (PTF)

Invariably these are the older generation who have watched every game at any one particular club for in excess of fifty years, can still remember young lads who were going to 'make it' until 'she came along' and can recall the day that the storm of '52 blew the weather vane clean off the pavilion roof straight onto 'oh you remember? That umpire. Big bloke? Wore glasses. Broke wind at the end of every over.'

This set of PTFers loiter around the tea and, once they have decided that everyone has had enough, they pounce. Well, not pounce as such, more lean in gently to the table, sometimes swaying, occasionally stumbling, often not bothering with plates and using the tea as a personal afternoon finger buffet. And their evening meal. Sometimes even tomorrow's breakfast as well, especially if the day is cold and their winter coats with the voluminous pockets are still in active service.

Bear in mind this set have not paid match fees. Also remember that they prop up the bar at close of play and probably pour more money into the till than most other club members. Perhaps a quarter of a gently curling tuna and raisin sandwich isn't too shabby a reward for their years of dedication to the club's cause and coffers.

Village Club Scorers

A distinct grouping that usually bring their own food as even a minute away from the pristine scorebook, iPad and safety blanket roll of twenty differently coloured pens makes a nosebleed highly possible and a full faint probable.

A tower of flapjacks will revive the match scorers. Scorers are a rare breed – cherish them.

Their own cricket tea will include a healthy salad or leftovers from the previous evening's meal. Scorers are like that. However, every cricketer knows that this is not enough to sustain them through what is the only position on and around a cricket field that demands 100 per cent concentration throughout the day. Scorers are also a rare breed and need to be cherished. A low-rise tower block of flapjack cubes around the twenty-over mark will do the trick.

Some experienced scorers have the confidence to join in with the cricket family and take tea with everyone else. This doesn't happen a lot. But if they do that roll of coloured pens will be housed in an adapted bum-bag, thus limiting the number of almond slices that can be taken on board for later use. Therefore, ensure that the oat-based pick-me-up is to hand. It will be needed if you want to know the factual result of the game.

My Favourite Cricket Tea

Luke Fletcher is a local legend in his home county. Born in Nottingham, he played his club cricket locally and made his first class debut for Nottinghamshire in 2008.

Luke's spells of devastatingly accurate bowling are always eagerly anticipated by spectators and teammates alike.

With over 300 first class wickets and seventy-plus T20 wickets to his name, he's the go-to bowler for any Nottinghamshire captain in every form of the game. He's also handy with the bat, crashing more than 2,000 runs in first class matches. Luke describes himself as 'friendly, big and hungry' – having an appetite for his team's success and for a good cricket tea.

NOTTINGHAMSHIRE
COUNTY CRICKET CLUB ®

Luke Fletcher, local hero and devastating bowler. Handy with the bat as well.

Sustained bowling spells require top-class nutrition.

Killamarsh Juniors
Cricket Club in
Derbyshire holds fond
memories for Luke.

When I was younger playing in the Notts Premier League, I can remember a brilliant cricket tea up at Killamarsh in North East Derbyshire. They brought ten or so big bags of chips and loads of curry sauce and bread and butter. Fantastic.

At county grounds I do like it at Trent Bridge and Leicestershire is always a good tea. But Lords is special. I couldn't believe the first time I went there. Fridges full of soft drinks, a dressing room attendant who would go and get bacon cobs if you asked and sometimes three course meals.

And standing at 6 feet 6 inches, nutrition is vital to this medium fast bowler.

For bowlers there is nothing better than getting a team out just before tea. That way you know you can tuck in without the worry of having to bowl again or bat for a day or so.

6

Putting the T in Victory

A cricket tea can be as simple as sprinkling pre-grated processed cheese between two slices of bread and emptying popcorn into a bowl. Ta-dah, tea is served. It will after all fill a gap, allow players to rest and gets the job done. It's also cheap. But it's hardly the stuff of memories and nostalgia.

One cricket-crazy chef feels a tea is much more than simple sustenance. Tommy Banks is the chef at The Black Swan in Oldstead, North Yorkshire. He also happens to be Britain's youngest Michelin-starred chef (awarded in 2013) and won BBC *Great British Menu* in 2016 and 2017. The Black Swan was awarded 'The Best Restaurant in the UK 2018' by *The Food and Travel Magazine* and the 'Best Fine Dining Restaurant in the World' by TripAdvisor in 2017.

Tommy obviously knows about food but is also an avid cricket player and fan, having in his younger playing days pitted his skills against equally talented lads such as Jonny Bairstow (who may be a much-loved international cricketer with thousands of runs to his name, but can he rustle up langoustine skewers with caramelised whey between the fall of the third and fourth wickets in a match at Easingwold?).

Tommy has also played for the Tailenders team in a match against BBC *Test Match Special* at Derbyshire in 2018. He scored eighteen off a Phil Tufnell over, totalled thirty-three with the bat and returned bowling figures of 4–2.

'It was amazing. When I was batting I kept looking up at the screen to see the replays of the shots. OK, one or two squirted through slips but it doesn't say that in the scorebook. What an experience.' As was being interviewed by Jonathan Agnew for 'View from the Boundary' on *Test Match Special* in August 2018. It's therefore a massive understatement to say that Tommy quite likes his cricket.

As a thirteen-year-old, Tommy was playing around Yorkshire at various representative matches and had a definite favourite sandwich.

Egg mayo was the best. But at one match I picked out a handful of what I thought were egg mayo to find, after one mouthful, that they were cheese and onion. I couldn't put them back as that's against all the etiquette of a cricket tea. What a

Above left: So much to concentrate on. Even the score.

Above right: Tommy Banks, award-winning chef. He also likes a bit of cricket. Maybe he just likes wearing white?

The Black Swan at Oldstead, North Yorkshire, Tommy's award-winning restaurant.

mistake by me and by whoever put onion in a sandwich. It was great chunks of onion and that's a definite no-no. Onion doesn't half repeat on you and that can be uncomfortable when bowling off a long run up.

Cakes though are important in a cricket tea. Lots of players fill up on cake. It's wrong but somehow right at the same time. No other sport has such a bad diet than most club cricketers on match day. It's mainly carbohydrates and sugar but, well, it's cricket isn't it?

Tommy's cricket experiences continued when playing in the Yorkshire Premier League.

I was practising five times a week, playing matches and it was too much to do along with the restaurant. I now only play Wednesdays and that's T20 games.

But cricket teas at weekends were always so good. They are pure nostalgia as well. In most sports it's all isotonic drink and stuff at the interval. But with cricket it's different. You can't beat a mug of hot tea after playing in the sun for a few hours or weak orange cordial in plastic beakers. It's resulted in me having a plastic beaker of the stuff in the kitchen when I'm preparing food for the restaurant. The taste immediately takes me back to the cricket field.

For someone who is fabulous at creating recipes and dishes, Tommy has relatively simple tastes when it comes to a cricket tea.

I like the individual cakes you get. Jam tarts, Battenberg and Bakewell slices. You can easily reach over the table to get one or two; they are easy to handle especially if you have a plate in one hand and a mug of tea in the other. If you can eat it in one go then it has to be good.

Larger slices of cake can often fall apart when you lift them onto your plate so homemade isn't always the best for a cricket tea. I do think that crisps are a cop out though. And there's no place for cold pizza on a cricket tea table.

Scones are a different matter altogether. They have to be there. And it's fair to say that the 'third rule' applies to scones: a third scone, a third jam and a third cream. But the scone has to be good. They are after all the vehicle for the jam and cream.

And that, remember, is Michelin-starred advice.

However, not all sandwich fillings are used between bread. Tommy, aged seventeen, was playing for the York league representative side against Huddersfield and, like for so many cricket fans of the day, Andrew Flintoff was a bit of a hero.

Flintoff always strode to the crease, cricket helmet in hand so that he could stare at the opposition and they could see that he wasn't intimidated in any way. Tommy took this habit on board and duly strode to the crease, cricket helmet in hand, before placing it on his head, taking guard and beginning what he hoped would be a spectacular match-winning innings.

Above: Simple jam tarts are all that Tommy wants from a cricket tea.

Left: Crisps? 'No,' says Tommy. 'A bit of a cop out.'

Orange juice in the restaurant kitchen reminds Tommy of his cricket days out in the sun.

What Tommy didn't know was that his teammates had smeared tuna mayonnaise on the inside of the helmet and as the heat of the day picked up and combined with the sweat of the toiling Tommy, the gelatinous sandwich filling turned to a fishy liquid.

That's no way to treat a staple sandwich filling, nor, for that matter, an aspiring batsman and someone who went on to gain prestigious awards for his culinary skills.

Rocky Road to Love

India Felton – along with her mum, Sancha Hopkins – has been making cricket teas at the fabulous Newtown Linford Cricket Club in Leicestershire for seven years. The club is celebrating its centenary in 2019 with plenty of exciting activity both on and off the playing field, but it was back in 2015 when cheers echoed around the ground as the club won the Great Cricket Tea Challenge, sponsored by Yorkshire Tea.

It was so exciting and I couldn't believe it when we won. The final was pressurised with top players and a panel of judges, including Mike Gatting.

I've been involved with the teas with my mum ever since we stood in for a tea lady who couldn't make a particular week. That was back in 2012. We've been doing it full time ever since. My grandma always baked, my mum is a great cook so I just joined in. It was the best way to see each other at the weekends when the rest of the family were playing in the matches.

Cricket teas have had a massive impact on my life as I actually met my husband over a tea. There was one match where I had made Rocky Road and after the game he managed to get my phone number and called, asking for the recipe. We got married in late 2018.

Cricket teas are vital to the game as they really bring people together, as I well know, and in the break in the game players can calm down and become human again. Cricket teas are embedded at club level.

Nowadays, I only make the teas for the first team with my brother's girlfriend making the others. After making so many over the years, I would always recommend preparing some the night before the match and make sure everything is easy to pick off the plate. Cricketers can be impatient as they only have twenty minutes or so to have the tea. And I think that all sandwiches should be ready assembled, scones should be pre-jammed, and avoid anything too heavy. They still have a few hours to play after tea.

I don't bother with salads and healthy stuff as our teams don't seem to want them and I try to make everything myself. Homemade pizza, cheese straws, pies, garlic bread, cakes, brownies, flapjacks, homemade chicken nuggets always go down well and, of course, Rocky Road.

Above left: Newtown Linford Cricket Club in Leicestershire produces award-winning cricket teas.

Above right: Sancha Hopkins makes everything herself in a Newtown Linford Cricket Club tea.

Home-made cakes are essential in award-winning cricket teas.

It's so much more than a simple cricket tea cake.

My Favourite Cricket Tea

Abbi Aitken became Scotland women's captain at nineteen years old and is a super-talented all-rounder. Like many of today's top cricketers, Abbi's first experience of the sport was in Kwik Cricket.

Abbi developed through the age groups and made her international debut for Scotland in 2018. Abbi is well placed to judge both club and international level teas. She doesn't hold back.

Most of my memories of cricket teas probably relate back to my early years playing the game where I started out at Montrose Cricket Club. I have many a fond memory of cricket teas – not fond because of the memorable delights on offer, however.

As we all know, lower league cricket heavily relies on its volunteers within our clubs and the creation and service of our cricket teas most definitely does. Home teas at my club required each player bringing "tea for two" as we called it. Not the best organisation, but you hoped that not everyone would turn up with the same savouries or similar fillings, but it was always quite entertaining to see what the result was and which of your team mates committed the ultimate crime of cutting their sandwiches into rectangles and not the classic triangle.

I clearly remember one of the youngsters turning up to his first senior game having been asked to take tea for two. He arrived with a large flask of tea but to be fair to him, it did contain enough for two.

Another memory would be playing against what I recall was the Duke of Fife and his team, Brigadier Duncan's XI. It was a friendly match that I'm sure only happened once a year. But I remember it because even though it was always a home friendly, they always supplied the teas.

Abbi Aitken, former captain of Scotland women's national team, knows what's good and bad in a cricket tea.

Taking the first ball after tea can influence what's on a teatime plate.

It has to be triangles. Every time and no excuses.

One or two lemon slices is fine. But hundreds?

There was a superb array of sandwiches and goodies on offer, but the sandwich I remember picking from the selection was cucumber and sugar. I've never seen such a combination since. Nor have I ever come round to liking cucumber.

I also recall bowling a team out for less than one hundred away from home – a rare feat for the mighty Montrose regardless if we played home or away. And at the innings break, we weren't offered any teas – they just fed themselves.

At more senior level, I've had the pleasure of travelling the length and breadth of the UK to play matches. For me, a healthier, lighter option goes down well and I do love it when clubs offer up a 'make your own' style lunch. As an opening bowler and a tailender, what gets plated up is often dictated by what's happened in the first innings. The nightmare scenario is coming in to teas having faced out the last few overs and knowing I'll be taking first ball. I barely have time to look at the teas, never mind critique them.

My ideal cricket tea menu is a hot option, cold alternatives (a pasta salad for example), breads, meats and cheeses (build your own sarnie), salads, yoghurt and fruit. And if I can convince myself to take a little treat it's got to be the classic scone, strawberry jam and clotted cream combo for me.

There is nothing worse than walking towards a cricket tea table and seeing a sea of beige. White bread sandwiches with lack of filling, perhaps a tray of chicken nuggets, sausage rolls and some pakora, bhajis, spring rolls and other frozen oven 'delights'. Unfortunately, it has been a far too common sight over the years.

I also may be slightly controversial here too but as much as I enjoy a sweet treat, I don't like to see the classic array of cakes and biscuits at the end of the table. Maybe I'm scarred from turning up to a game in my youth where the opposition had obviously had a severe lack of tea coordination which resulted in us being offered two hundred Mr Kipling lemon cakes for tea. Nothing else.

And that's tea.

Acknowledgements

The author and publisher would like to thank the following people and organisations for permission to use copyright material in this book: unsplash.com; Sir Michael Parkinson; Michael Vaughan OBE; The Roger Mann Picture Library; Trent Bridge Library; Cricket Scotland; Clifton Alliance Cricket Club; Vilma Buck; Uffington Cricket Club; Annie Chave; The Erratics Cricket Club; Armadillos Cricket Club; Jo Shaw; Stella Deam; Southport & Birkdale Cricket Club; Sandwich Town Cricket Club; Yorkshire Tea; Simon Stacpoole/Offside; Papplewick and Linby Cricket Club; Glynis Culley; Patrick Latham; Durham County Cricket Club; Kevin Howells; Stephen Chalke; John Russell; Fleckney Village Cricket Club; Lancashire County Cricket Club; Jack Simmons MBE; Mark Leech; Woodbridge Cricket Club; Huw Turbervill; Michelle Woods; Yorkshire County Cricket Club; Nottinghamshire County Cricket Club; Tommy Banks; Newtown Linford Cricket Club; Sancha Hopkins and India Felton.

Every attempt has been made to seek permission for copyright material used in this book. However, if we have inadvertently used copyright material without permission or acknowledgement we apologise and we will make the necessary correction at the first opportunity.

With Thanks

Many people have been incredibly helpful in the making of this book. Amberley Publishing took the plunge and commissioned the book. Good for them.

Every cricket club included in the book have willingly provided tea tales and photographs, and for that I thank you. Special thanks goes to Eastwood Town Cricket Club in Nottinghamshire for allowing many of the photographs used in the book to be taken in their pavilion. The County Cricket Clubs included in the book have been marvellous, as have County Cricket Club libraries and players.

Cricket Scotland was helpful way above and beyond my requests.

Sir Michael Parkinson is officially a national treasure.

Sue Gibbins provided essential and invaluable editing guidance and Ian Ward produced a marvellous cover.

Mark Scott is an unbelievable talent when wielding a camera. Mark is the most creative photographer I have ever met. I cannot thank him enough for his efforts.

Above all, I would like to thank Catherine, Jack and Freddie. The boys ensure that cricket is ever-present in my life and Catherine's unswerving support is truly humbling. Catherine also bakes rather tasty cakes.